Why I Can't Say
I Love You

Why I Can't Say
I Love You

Jack Balswick

WORD BOOKS
PUBLISHER
WACO, TEXAS

Library of Congress catalog card number: 77–92472
ISBN 0–8499–0079–4
Printed in the United States of America

Unless otherwise noted, all Scripture quotations are from the Revised Standard Version of the Bible, copyright © 1946, 1952, © 1971, 1973 by the Division of Christian Education of the National Council of the Churches of Christ in the United States of America, and are used by permission.

Quotations from *The New English Bible* (NEB), © The Delegates of The Oxford University Press and The Syndics of The Cambridge University Press, 1961, 1970, are reprinted by permission.

Quotations from *The New American Standard Bible* (NAS) are © The Lockman Foundation 1960, 1962, 1968, 1971.

TO MY MOTHER AND FATHER
WHOSE LOVE I'VE NEVER DOUBTED

Contents

Preface

WHAT I HAVE to say in this book is based both on personal experience and academic research. I grew up as one who had a hard time sharing his feelings with others. Saying "I love you" was, for me, harder than running five miles before breakfast. It was out of this personal frustration of having feelings but not being able to share them, that I became interested in researching the conditions which contribute to what I have called "the inexpressive male" syndrome.

Since this book is partly based upon my own experience, it will reflect a man's point of view. Thus I will have more to say on why husbands can't say "I love you" than on wives. In my chapter on why parents can't say "I love you," I will have more to say about fathers than mothers. I also believe, however, that men in our society actually *do* have more trouble expressing their feelings to others.

I firmly believe that the human personality can change. We do ourselves a disservice when we think that we were born with a certain personality type which determines the way we respond to others. We human beings are dynamic, adaptable, and capable of great change, including our ability to express ourselves to those we care about. At one point I thought of myself as an inexpressive male who didn't want to be that way. Although I have a long way to go, as I have become more able to share my feelings with others, I have found life to be more fulfilling for me as a husband, a father, a friend, and a teacher.

1

The Importance of Saying
"I Love You"

SOME YEARS AGO there was a popular song entitled, "Three Little Words." The three little words which the singer wishes to hear are "I love you."

The song expressed a universal longing. Somehow it is terribly important to all of us that we hear these words. Why is that? And why is it important for others to hear these words from us? Why is it so important to do something that is so difficult to do—to say "I love you"?

This whole book tries to answer these questions. I want to talk about the importance of love—both experiencing and expressing it—and about the barriers we erect to prevent our doing both.

It is ironic that what ought to be the most effortless and pleasurable phrase to say to another person—"I love you"—winds up being one of the most difficult. Surely it is easy to understand why we wouldn't want to say "I hate you" to someone. That is difficult and unpleasant. But to say "I love you"? Such a statement should flow with a natural ease from our inner reservoir of feelings.

We know that nothing would make those we love happier than to hear an expression of our love. And yet, we feel strangely uncomfortable just thinking about communicating love. It seems so effortless to be passionate about expressing our thoughts and feelings on politics, or sports, or even religion. But to express our love freely to another person? Well, that's something else! Why do we need to talk about that? Shouldn't some things just be taken for granted?

It isn't that we don't have feelings of love towards the persons we are closest to. We do feel love towards our spouse, our children, our parents, our close friends. We do not doubt that the feelings are there. In fact they are often the most certain feelings we have. But to communicate those feelings verbally is difficult indeed. Again we are forced to question: How is it that something so difficult to express is at the same time so important?

The Importance of Expressing Love in Alternative Ways

It is with relief that we consider alternative ways of expressing love. As with our other emotions, we are not limited to verbal means of expression. Our feelings for another person can be communicated in a number of ways—through "body language," overt physical behavior, symbolic gestures, and written language.

We are often unaware of the ways in which our body language communicates to others. Our eyes, lips, face, posture, and general body movement all do a great deal to express what we are feeling. Research conducted on small discussion groups has even discovered that open- or closed-mindedness is communicated through body language. A person who assumes an open and relaxed body posture is likely to be open-minded about the ideas being discussed in the group. The group member who sits stiffly upright, tense, with legs crossed and arms folded, is likely to be closed-minded and defensive about the ideas which the group is discussing.

A skilled reader of body language can tell much about how a person is feeling without a word being spoken. People in intimate relationships, such as husbands and wives, may become very adept at reading the meaning of a glance, a touch, or a tender look given by the other.

But the problem with body language is that although it can express love, an ambiguous message can result when that is the only avenue of expression.

Love can also be communicated through more overt physical means—through a hug, a kiss, a pat on the back or derrière. A few years ago I was studying marriage relationships among Greeks in Cyprus. One of the questions I asked Greek wives was how often their husbands said "I love you" to them. Although all wives said that their husbands never told them this, the importance of overt physical expression of love was summed up in the response of one wife in her thirties— "Greek men are men of action, not men of words!" Parenthetically, it may be noted that most wives who were interviewed indicated that they wished that their husbands would also *tell* them of their love.

Love may also be communicated through symbolic

gestures—the giving of a dozen roses, a ring, a card, or two tickets to Hawaii! Here the object given represents the love and affection of the giver. Symbolic gestures will be a normal and expected part of most intimate relationships.

Love can be expressed in literary form through the writing of a letter, a poem, or a song. Although they are disastrous as poetic art forms, my wife still cherishes the love poems which I have written to her. It is often easier to express love in written form than in personal verbal interaction. Most intimate relationships would probably profit from more attempts to express love in writing. This could also serve to encourage verbal communication of love at later stages.

Are these nonverbal forms of communicating love sufficient? Can feelings of love be effectively communicated by these media? If we find the verbal expression of affection difficult, we are tempted to answer yes. I believe, however, that the verbal communication of love possesses two qualities which are not combined in any of the above communication media: (1) preciseness in communication; and (2) personalness in communication.

Body language, overt physical behavior, and symbolic gestures may allow for personalness in communication, but they lack a degree of preciseness which characterizes verbal communication. Body language, for example, can be misread—"What does that gleam in his eye really mean?" Physical expressions can be misinterpreted—"Is he interested in me as a person or just my body?" Symbolic expression may be questioned—"Why

did he send me these flowers? What has he done now?"
Although a high degree of precision is obtained in
written communication, personalness is made more difficult. Expressing love through writing makes a simul-
taneous exchange of communication difficult. By their
very nature, written expressions of love are usually
intended for reading while the writer is not present.

I am not suggesting that verbal communication is
immune from misinterpretation, nor that it cannot be
used as a means of insincere expressions of love. I am
only suggesting that feelings such as love and affection
may be communicated most completely, personally, and
precisely by verbal means.

The complexity and multidimensionality of love has
been compared to the many-sidedness of a finely cut
diamond. Such a diamond can be appreciated in its
entirety only from many angles. Each angle will give
a different view and show a different facet of the unique
beauty of the diamond, and yet the diamond is one.
The same may be said for love. The depth and dimensions of love are best communicated by body language,
physical expressions, symbolic gestures, writing, and
verbal communication—all of them. Although all expressions of love are important, it is in the verbal encounter that human intimacy can most accurately be
experienced.

The Important Effects of Expressing Love

Why is it so important to express love? The expression of love is the cement which maintains intimacy in
close relationships. It has important effects upon the

person who expresses the love, upon the person who is the recipient of the expressed love, and upon the relationship between the two persons involved.

ON THE LOVER

An individual who is emotionally restricted often wants to but can't divulge his feelings to others. Others may have feelings but think it is a sign of weakness to express these feelings. The personal tragedy of this type of emotional inexpressiveness was brought home to me clearly one Saturday afternoon while my wife and I were attending a performance of Shakespeare's *Romeo and Juliet*. The roles of Romeo and Juliet were being played by sixteen-year-old young people; thus, the matinée performance was crowded with high school students. At the very tragic and serious death scene, when my wife and I had lumps in our throats and tears in our eyes, we were surprised to hear the sniffs of most females accompanied by loud guffaws from the adolescent boys. Obviously, the emotional impact was being sidetracked and expressed in a reactional manner to cover up the sad and tender emotions which were not "cool" for adolescent males to express.

It can be physically and psychologically unhealthy for a person to not release and express emotions. Physically, the inability to cry and express emotions is thought to be related to the development of ulcers. Psychologically, the holding in of emotions can result in a person's not being in touch with his feelings, and therefore becoming out of touch with himself. Articulating feelings helps us become aware of and recognize them. When we do not articulate what we feel, there is an uncertainty about the feelings. Just as talking over a problem with someone is a way to get a better understanding of that problem, so, articulating emotions forces us to conceptualize what is being felt.

ON THE LOVED

Another reason why it is so important to express love is that when we don't the person we love is deprived of hearing expressions of love. Hearing an "I love you" is more important than just the good feelings it produces on the inside. All of us need to hear and receive overt expressions of love from the time we are born. If a baby does not receive expressions of love during the first year of life, he or she may be unable to receive or express love during his or her entire lifetime.

There is a disease known as marrasmus (wasting away) which was common among infants who were war victims or poorly cared for in orphanages. Marrasmus is far more prevalent among children kept in orphanages than among orphaned children placed in foster homes. A child with marrasmus doesn't develop socially, psychologically or physically, and often wastes away and dies. What is most important for our purposes is the cause of marrasmus. It is not caused by food or material deprivation, but rather from the deprivation of love. Marrasmus develops when infants are not picked up, held, cuddled, caressed, kissed, hugged, squeezed, and generally loved.

None of us ever outgrows our need for receiving affection and love. As we mature from infancy to adulthood, we develop an increasing need for receiving verbal expressions of love, while retaining our need for physical expressions of love.

Have you ever considered how we learn to love ourselves? One of the most documented truths about child development is that a child develops a view of himself based on his perception of how others view him. It is no wonder that a boy who has been told repeatedly that he is "dumb" or "stupid," or a girl that she is "bad," "no good," "worthless," or "useless," come to view themselves in just these terms. Conversely, children who love themselves do so because their parents have both shown and verbally expressed their love. We come to love ourselves because others have expressed their love for us.

Unfortunately, all of us fail at some point to communicate love, particularly to our children, and most of us experience doubts about being loved, because of lacks in our childhood. Ultimately, there is only one person who is consistent in expressing and giving love—and that is God. And the good news is that God does love us. We will consider the implications of this in detail in the last chapter. But here let me say that because God loves us and has demonstrated that love to us, we can love ourselves. That this should be normative is reflected in Jesus' statement that we should love our neighbor as ourselves. The fact of the matter is that we can't love our neighbor unless we love ourselves. And loving ourselves is dependent upon grasping and experiencing others' love for us. The Apostle John sums this up when he says, "We love, because he first loved us." We love, because God loves and also because we have experienced the love other people have for us. God's loving us is the supreme example of why it is important to hear the message from others, "I love you."

THE LOVE RELATIONSHIP

Lastly, the expression of love from one person to another is important for the love relationship. A social relationship consists of a bond between two persons who take each other into account. Intimate love relationships are based upon *commitment* and maintained by *communication.*

Although the emotions may be involved in love, more than anything else love is a commitment. The apostle Paul describes this kind of love in his letter to the church at Corinth—love "bears all things, believes all things, hopes all things, endures all things. . . . Love never fails" (1 Cor. 13:7–8).

A commitment involves both rights and responsibilities. From the point of view of the recipient of a commitment, rights are involved. From the point of view of the person giving the commitment, responsibility is involved. True love relationships are always reciprocal and mutual—two-way, not one-way. Each person experiences the relationship as involving both rights and responsibilities. When love is present in a marriage relationship, the husband experiences his wife's love and care as a right, while the wife experiences her loving and caring as her responsibility. Because the love relationship is mutual, the wife experiences her husband's love and care as a right, while the husband experiences his loving and caring as his responsibility.

In the same way that mutual commitment is the *basis* of a love relationship, so mutual communication is the *process* whereby a love relationship is maintained and enhanced. A love relationship does not grow where there is only one-way communication. In a relationship with only one-way communication, only one person is attempting to express personal feelings to the other. At best, one-way communication may keep a love relationship alive. At worst, one-way communication is unable to sustain a love relationship.

The expressive person often makes valiant efforts to sustain the love relationship, while the inexpressive member of the relationship is either unwilling or unable to express his or her feelings. In many marriages where this is the case, the expressive spouse will pretend that everything in the relationship is all right, that nothing is wrong with the relationship. Some even rationalize that this is the way a marriage relationship should be, that an open, emotionally sharing relationship is impossible to sustain over time. The wife who has an inexpressive husband may find it especially easy to rationalize—"Men are just that way; they just don't talk about their feelings."

One-way communication can stagnate a love relationship in several additional ways. When one person expresses feelings and never gets any feedback, the lack of responsiveness serves as a kind of negative reinforcement. The expressive person begins to express less and less. The depths we are able to achieve in relationships with our friends depend very much on the extent to which the sharing of our feelings is reciprocated.

Another result of one-way communication is a lack of security. When someone never tells us about his feelings for us, we soon wonder where we stand with him. Such insecurity often produces rather devious types of manipulative behavior which are designed to evoke some kind of positive response from the inexpressive person.

At this point, it may be wise to draw back a bit and consider the relevance to one-way communication of the nonverbal types of communication we discussed earlier in this chapter. You may be asking, "Can't body language, physical behavior, or symbolic gestures be used to elevate a seemingly one-way communication to a two-way communicative relationship?" The simpler answer is, "Yes, this is possible." But an additional question to ask is, "How far can any of these nonverbal types of communication carry a love relationship?" The answer to this question is a more complex one. If one member of the love relationship is communicating only by nonverbal means, then it is imperative that the other member of the relationship be able to read the often hidden meaning in the nonverbal messages. When a conscious effort is made, the expressive person may be quite successful in interpreting the "real meaning" in a bodily, physical, or symbolic gesture. A grunt, sigh, cough, or glance may carry significant messages to the skilled interpreter who has spent a lifetime deciphering the wishes and feelings of the inexpressive partner.

However, such relationships almost inevitably lack

a depth and richness which can only be cultivated by the free, mutual, verbal sharing of feelings. We are beings who hunger for reassurance from others that they love and care about us. Most of us want and need assurance delivered in unambiguous ways.

So far, our discussion has centered upon love relationships in which at least one member was verbally expressive. In relationships where neither member is verbally expressive, the communication of love is even more difficult. Some relationships may be this way from their inception. In others, one of the partners was initially verbally expressive, but became inexpressive because of the unresponsiveness of the other. A love relationship void of verbal communication of love and affection is possible. However, the most vital means of maintaining intimacy in the relationship is missing. The unambiguous communication of love is important to the lover, the loved, and the love relationship; it is the catalyst which advances intimacy in relating and independence of being for two who love each other.

2

Why I Can't Say
"I Love You"

I GREW UP as a typical inexpressive male—a person who found it difficult to say, "I love you." It was certainly not the case that I didn't have feelings—I did. However, to tell someone else verbally how I was feeling was another thing.

Fortunately, the woman I married was a vibrant, responsive woman who was willing to draw me out. She encouraged me to examine the uncomfortable struggle I had over expressing personal things. "I wonder why you don't talk about your feelings more?" she asked. "I know you feel very strongly about things, but you seldom reveal this to anyone."

It began to dawn on me that I was missing an intimacy with others by keeping my feelings bottled, and the effort was taking its toll on me. Being a sociologist, I became interested in trying to understand the circumstances and events which caused this struggle.

This male inexpressiveness is no triviality; it's a real

tragedy for the man's wife, his children, and most especially, for the man himself. Think of the wife who,
year after year, never hears the words "I love you."
Consider the child who is never told, "Fine work, I'm
proud of you." And think of the tragedy of the man
himself, crippled by an inability to express this part of
himself—his warm and tender feelings for other people.

Although we men are often thought to have the most
difficulty in demonstrating our love, the practice of
keeping feelings bottled up is not limited to us. You
may be married to a woman who has trouble saying
"I love you." You may be the spouse who has trouble
telling your mate of your love, or the one who has come
to keep your feelings to yourself because your verbal
expressions of affection are never returned. You may
be a parent who would like the freedom to express love
to your children. Perhaps your own parents are getting
older and have more need for being told that they are
loved and wanted, but you find it difficult to express the
love you feel. Or, you may have a very close friend
whom you really care about, but you find yourself feeling very uncomfortable just thinking about openly
communicating your love and caring. Why do we have
this problem? My concern is to uncover the possible
reasons why we do not say "I love you" to those whom
we love.

Fear

Could it be that we actually fear telling others what
they would most like to hear from us? Surely that could
not be true. It makes no sense to fear expressing love

to someone else. But then, maybe much of what we do doesn't seem to make much sense when we stop to think about it. Regardless of how irrational it seems, we sometimes do not say "I love you" because of fear.

Consider Jim and Joanie, who have been married for ten years. They have a babysitter watching their two children for the evening while they are out enjoying a candlelight dinner. The dinner was great; they are relaxing as they finish their coffee and dessert. As the light from the candle flickers across Joanie's face, Jim notices how beautiful she is and realizes how much he loves her. He has the urge to reach across the table, grab her hand and tell her how much he loves her. But, instead of following this impulse, he hesitates. The evening passes with Jim's never having said what he feels. What type of fear does Jim's hesitation possibly reflect?

Sally and Marie have been friends for five years. They have shared many experiences together since they first met in the maternity ward at the births of their first children. Since then they have often visited together, comparing notes on the development of their children. For the past week while Sally has been sick with the flu, Marie has cleaned her house, cooked dinners, and taken care of her child. Now that Sally is well, she wants to tell Marie how much she appreciates all that she has done for her while she was ill. She does and then has the urge to tell Marie also how much she loves her. But the expression of her appreciation stops short of this, and she departs for home never telling Marie of the love she feels for her.

What type of fear caused Sally not to say "I love you"?

When we express our love to another person, we open ourselves up to that person. It is not just our own feelings we are revealing, but our feelings *for* the other person. When we intimately share our feelings of love for another, we often feel vulnerable. It is as if we are emotionally naked, as if we have stripped off all that is superficial and allowed another to see our bare emotions. When we have placed ourselves in this state, we begin to fear that our expression of love will be rejected, or that it will be ignored, or not acknowledged, or not returned. These are some of the fears associated with expressing our love for another.

Fear of expressing love can also be understood as the risk of being hurt. If I tell you that I love you, and you laugh at me, then I will feel hurt. As a matter of fact, if I tell you that I love you, and you merely don't respond, I may feel hurt.

Even when we are reasonably sure that an expression of love will be returned, we hesitate. Although such hesitation may make no sense in a present situation, the experience of expressing love in the past and being rewarded by unresponsiveness is perhaps still in our memory.

Low Self-Esteem

Although the fear of expressing love is in part a symptom of low self-esteem, in a broader sense low self-esteem can also inhibit us from saying "I love you."

A person with low self-esteem believes that he or she has no love to give. Such a person views him- or herself as not worthwhile—as not possessing the quality of love which someone else would be glad to receive.

Where self-esteem is extremely low, there may also be an inability to love oneself. When self-love is difficult, then even loving someone else is difficult. The person with a low self-esteem may find it difficult to love others, and even when love is present, to express that love to others.

Embarrassment

Another fear which can inhibit us from expressing love is embarrassment. We anticipate that we will be embarrassed when we say "I love you" to another person. This may be especially true in a relationship which has existed for some time and yet love has never been expressed. When certain patterns of communication have been established, we feel awkward attempting to develop new ways of communicating. Parents who have told their children that they love them from the time they were born generally have no embarrassment about communicating this love when their children are grown. Parents who have not established such a pattern of expressiveness may feel embarrassed about beginning verbal expressions of love when their children are grown. Although grown children may want to tell aging parents of their love, even pondering such an expression is embarrassing when it has never been done before.

Not Enough Time

The nurturing which love relationships need takes time. We rarely just blurt out our feelings of love to another. Instead, feelings of love are usually uttered in the context of a personal sharing of ourselves with another. Merely to say "I love you" doesn't take time, but the cultivation of the intimacy within which love can be expressed comfortably does take time. The expression of love will more likely be a forced activity, if it does occur, in a relationship in which the participants have not invested a part of themselves and their time in each other.

Talking About Trivia

Merely being verbal is not being expressive. Some people have the ability to talk and talk and talk, but they never express their feelings. It is possible to talk about all kinds of trivia with one we love, and in so doing leave little time for the expression of feelings. In reality, continual chatter may even be a defense mechanism which serves to keep a person from communicating on the feeling level.

Intellectualization

Talking about trivia is not the only defense against communicating on the feeling level. Another is the practice of intellectualizing feelings. Some people become very skilled at analyzing or talking about feelings, and in so doing never express their own feelings. When asked the straightforward question, "Do you love me?" the intellectualizer is likely to respond, "It seems to be very important for you to know—why do you question my love for you? The quality of my love for you is mature, and the quantity of my love is abundant." Such a person seems to be incapable of simply responding, "I love you." Instead the intellectualizer treats love as a topic to be discoursed on and analyzed.

Out of Touch with Feelings

Another reason why some people never express love is that they are not in touch with their feelings. To be in touch with one's feelings is to know what they are— to be able to identify feelings when they are present. People who are out of touch with their feelings may certainly "feel" emotions, but they have such a weak grasp of the nature of those emotions that they find it virtually impossible to express them. When such a person genuinely does attempt to express feelings towards a loved one, he or she is most likely to express them indirectly. The inexpressive husband who is feeling love towards his wife, but has trouble specifically identifying this feeling as love, may say, "I guess I knew what I was doing when I picked you." Such expressions are genuine and are certainly better than not saying anything at all. But because he is out of touch with his feelings, he can identify his emotional states merely as either positive or negative. When you ask such a person how he is feeling, he is likely to reply by either saying "good," or "bad," or "I don't know!" Such a person lacks a vital self-awareness which is necessary for engaging in continuing intimate relationships.

Big Boys Don't Cry

Males in our society may have more difficulty in saying "I love you" than females because of the way we raise children. In learning to be a man, the boy in our society comes to value so-called expressions of masculinity and devalue expressions of femininity. Masculinity is expressed largely through physical courage, toughness, competitiveness, and aggressiveness, whereas femininity is, in contrast, expressed largely through gentleness, expressiveness, and responsiveness. When a young boy begins to express his emotions through crying, his parents are quick to assert, "You're a big boy, and big boys don't cry," or "Don't be such a sissy," or "Try to be a man about it."

Parents often use the expression "He's all boy" in reference to their son, and this usually refers to behavior which is an expression of aggressiveness, getting into mischief, getting dirty, etc. They seldom use the term to denote behavior which is an expression of affection, tenderness, or love. Anger, boisterous humor, competitive or athletic enthusiasm, physical or verbal aggression, and similar emotions which are deemed to be "manly" are acceptable; but "feminine" emotions— tenderness, compassion, sentimentality, gentleness, verbal affection, soft-heartedness, and the like—are clearly to be avoided. What parents are really telling their son is that a "real man" does not show his emotions, and if he is a "real man," he will not allow his emotions to be expressed.

As the boy moves out from under the family umbrella

and into the sphere of male peer groups, the taboo against expressing any feeling characteristic of girls is reinforced and continued. To be affectionate, gentle and expressive towards others is not being "one of the boys." The mass media seem to convey a similar message. From comics and cartoons through the more "adult" fare, the male image does not usually include affectionate, gentle, tender, or soft-hearted behavior—unless it happens to come from a very small boy (for adults to appreciate, not as a model for other young boys), or from an old, gray-haired grandfather.

Family, peer group, and mass media, then, converge to set the tune to which the male must dance. Confronted with the image projected by this powerful triumvirate, most young males quickly learn that whatever masculine behavior *is,* it *is not* an expression of gentleness, tenderness, compassion, verbal affection or love.

There are many reasons why we don't say "I love you" to those we love and care about. With some, there may be only one main reason for our inability to express feelings of love. With others, inability to express feelings is a combination of several of the reasons discussed. Some of us will have difficulty expressing feelings to our spouse for one reason, to our children for another, and to our close friends for yet a third reason. The remaining part of this book will be devoted to considering the difficulties we can have in expressing love in various types of relationships. We will look at the reasons why the verbal expression of love is difficult, at the effects of

this inexpressiveness upon relationships and the persons
involved, and at possible ways in which we might open
up clogged channels of communication with those we
love.

3

Why Husbands Can't Say "I Love You"

ONE OF THE true tragedies of American life is the fact that so many American men—perhaps a majority, and certainly a large minority—choke on the words "I love you." They find it difficult, if not impossible, to tell the people they love the most what they really feel. These men, whom I have termed in my studies, "inexpressive males," are not cruel, unfeeling beasts who care for nobody. They do care, often very deeply, for their wives, their children, their friends and relatives. But most of the time, in most places, they find it impossible to communicate to the people around them what is really going on in their hearts.

Surely you recognize the typical American man. Perhaps he is a member of your family: your husband, your father—or yourself. He spends his evenings with the family not talking, but watching television, reading the paper, or working on his hobby. If you ask him, "How did it go at work today?" he responds, "Okay, same as usual." Or, hoping to involve him in a conversation,

you bring up the subject of the long weekend coming
up: what would he like to do? "Oh," he mumbles, "I
don't care—whatever you want to do."

Such a husband may spend much of his time watching
television, especially sports, and display quite passionate emotions in reaction to the plight of his favorite
sports team. He may spend much time with his hobbies
or playing golf or tennis, and become very expressive
in describing his interest in them. Two or three evenings
a week he may go out without his family to the bowling
alleys or the ballgame. Here, among his buddies, he
may be able to relax a little, to get off his chest his
problem with his boss, or his worries about his future—
or even his feelings for his wife and children.

For this man has his feelings of warmth and tenderness for his family. He'll tell his buddies, bursting with
pride, "My kid hit two homers yesterday," and go on
to describe how far the ball carried. He may even tell
them, in an off-hand way, how much he cares for his
wife: "She's a pretty good girl," he'll say. "I owe her
a lot." But he finds it difficult to say the same things to
the people who need to hear them the most. He is like
the old Vermonter, married forty years, who remarked,
"I love my wife so much, sometimes I can hardly keep
from telling her so."

A joke! Yes, but not to those involved. I was discussing this subject once with a friend of mine. He
nodded sadly. "That's me all over," he said. "I can't
talk to my wife, I can't talk to my kids." I know this
man cares deeply for his family; he spends a great deal
of time with them. But he can't open his heart to them.

And his wife is left to worry—do I really matter to him? His children wonder—does Daddy really think I'm okay? And he himself is deprived of the warmth of sharing in his own family.

Why do such men have difficulty sharing their love with the persons they love the most?

The Creation of the Inexpressive Husband

We have already referred to the fact that society in general—family, peer groups, and the mass media—discourages the expression of love and affection in the American male. Expressions of love and affection are generally stereotyped as "feminine" behavior, and what we sadly tell males in our society is that if they are to be "real men" they won't show their emotions.

The problem, essentially, is cultural. That is to say, boys growing up in America today learn very early that a "real man" doesn't vent his feelings. When his sister cries, she is comforted; when he cries, he is told, "Big boys don't cry." When his sister hugs her mother, she hugs back; when he hugs his father, his father shies away. He tracks mud across the rug, breaks a lamp, gets into a fight with a neighboring child; we sigh, but we say, "He's all boy"—something we never say when he writes a poem or picks some wild flowers for his mother. His teachers at school also tell him that boys don't cry. So do his peers. If he talks about his inner feelings, his friends look at him askance. If he gives up his baseball game to take his little sister to the beach, they taunt him. If he cries, they jeer. The movies and television programs he sees show him endless male

heroes brawling and shooting one another; rarely does
he come across a hero who is tender toward a friend
or loved one.

Difficulties in Relating to Females

As a child, I watched all of those gun-toting heroes
on movie and television screens. I saw other boys at
school taunted because they cried. By the time I was in
high school I, too, found it difficult to express myself,
and especially difficult to talk to a girl. Even though I
was an athlete and reasonably popular, I rarely carried
on an intimate conversation with a girl. Usually my
dates were in groups, where I would have other boys to
talk to about "male matters"—batting averages and
cubic capacity of automobile engines. When I found
myself alone with a girl, there was virtually no conversation unless she was talkative, or drew me out.

There are two kinds of inexpressive males. I have
called them the *cowboy* and the *playboy*. Historically
in the United States we have admired the cowboy as a
symbol of masculinity. This is the "John Wayne" type
who feels more comfortable around his horse than his
girl. (I don't mean that Wayne is necessarily this sort
of man; it is the roles he plays that reflect the cowboy
type.) As portrayed by Wayne in any one of his many
type-cast roles, the mark of a real man is not to show
any tenderness or affection toward girls, because his
culturally acquired male image dictates that such a
show of emotions would be distinctly unmanly. If he
does have anything to do with girls, it is on a man-to-
man basis: the girl is treated roughly (but not sadisti-

cally), with only a disguised hint of gentleness or
affection. He likes girls, of course, but when he is with
them his conversation runs mostly to "Yes ma'am" and
"No ma'am" as he twists his hat in his hands and shuffles
from one foot to the next. As Manville puts it: "The
on-screen John Wayne doesn't feel comfortable around
women. He does like them sometimes—God knows he's
not *queer*. But at the right time, and in the right place
—which he chooses. And always with his car/horse
parked directly outside, in/on which he will ride away
to his more important business back in Marlboro country." [1]

Alfred Auerback, a psychiatrist, has commented
more directly on the cowboy type. He describes the
American male's inexpressiveness with women as part
of the "cowboy syndrome." He quite rightly states that
"the cowboy in moving pictures has conveyed the image
of the rugged 'he-man,' strong, resilient, resourceful,
capable of coping with overwhelming odds. His attitude
toward women is courteous but reserved." [2] As the cowboy loved equally his girlfriend and his horse, so the
present day American male loves his car or motorcycle
and his girlfriend. Basic to both these descriptions is the
notion that the cowboy does have feelings toward women
but does not express them, since such expression would
conflict with his image of what a male is.

The *playboy type* has recently been epitomized in
Playboy magazine and by James Bond. Like the cowboy, he is resourceful and shrewd, and interacts with
his girlfriend with a certain detachment which is expressed as "playing it cool." Although in his relation-

ships with women Bond is more of a Don Juan, he still
treats women with an air of emotional detachment and
independence similar to that of the cowboy. The playboy departs from the cowboy, however, in that he is
"non-feeling." Bond and the playboy he caricatures are
in a sense "dead" inside. They have no emotional feelings towards women. John Wayne, on the other hand,
although unwilling and perhaps unable to express them,
does have feelings. Bond rejects women as women,
treating them as consumer commodities; Wayne puts
women on a pedestal. The playboy's relationship with
women represents the culmination of Erich Fromm's
description of a marketing oriented personality, where
a person comes to see both himself and others as persons
to be manipulated and exploited. Sexuality is reduced
to a packageable consumption item which the playboy
can handle because it demands no responsibility. The
woman, in the process, becomes reduced to a playboy
accessory. A successful "love affair" is one in which
the bed was shared, but the playboy emerges having
avoided any personal involvement or shared relationship
with the woman.

The playboy, then, is in part the old cowboy in modern dress. Instead of the crude mannerisms of John
Wayne, the playboy is a skilled manipulator of women,
knowing when to turn the lights down, what music to
play on the stereo, which drinks to serve, and what
topics of conversation to engage in. The likeness, however, is not complete; the playboy does not seem to care
for the women from whom he withholds his emotions.

Thus, two types of inexpressive males come to marriage: the inexpressive feeling man (the cowboy) and the inexpressive nonfeeling man (the playboy). Few playboy types, however, marry, and when they do, they manage to conjure up enough love to convince themselves that they really are "in love." Since most men really love the women they marry, inexpressive husbands are likely to be of the cowboy variety.

Why Husbands Today Are Expected to Say "I Love You"

In the past, a marriage was judged in terms of production—whether the husband was a good provider and the wife a good manager and mother. The cowboy type of husband was an ideal to strive for. If the husband was a good provider and protector of his wife and family, and if the wife was a good homemaker and mother to her children, chances were the marriage was thought to be successful.

But today we have a different ideal, one that places a heavy demand on the marriage relationship. We believe that partners in a marriage—indeed all members of a family—ought to be companions and friends as well as parents and children, husbands and wives. There are several reasons for this change.

The first reason is that many of the traditional tasks which a husband and wife were expected to do in the home are now being done by specialists, groups, and organizations outside the home. The husband no longer leads his family in growing their own food; rather, it is bought at the supermarket with the money he earns at a job away from home. And since he usually is not

at home twenty-four hours a day, policemen and fire-
men are the protectors of his home and family. A variety
of specialists—plumbers, television repairmen, appli-
ance repairmen, roofers, etc.—are hired to do the tasks
which the husband was expected to do in the past. Many
of the wife's heavy duties are being accomplished by
modern conveniences—automatic washing machines,
dryers, dishwashers, and an assortment of electrical
gadgets. The long hours spent in the kitchen in the
past are now reduced by a variety of ready-made foods,
microwave ovens, and the like. The decline in these
"task" type of activities for both husband and wife has
increased the expectation that husbands and wives are
to be companions and sources of affection for each other.

A second reason for the change in expectations is
that two or three generations ago, people tended to live
for long periods—often their whole lives—in one com-
munity, surrounded by family and old friends. There
might be grandparents, uncles, aunts, nephews, and
cousins in one town comprising one large extended
family. In practical terms this meant that wives had
plenty of people around to interact with—somebody
was there to share a joke with, to tell their troubles to,
to share their happiness. If the husband was inexpressive—well, there were other people as substitutes.

Today we no longer live in those large extended families. We are mobile, leaving friends and neighbors behind. More and more we have come, out of necessity, to
depend on the members of the immediate family for
affection, communication, and friendship. Husbands
and wives very often have nobody else to tell their joys

and sorrows to. The tragedy of the inexpressive male is therefore magnified, for more than ever his wife needs communication with him.

A third reason is that as American society has become increasingly mechanized and depersonalized, the family remains one of the few social groups where the "primary" relationship has still managed to survive. Therefore, a greater and greater demand has been placed upon the modern family and especially the modern marriage to provide for affection and companionship. Indeed, a highly plausible explanation for the increased rate of divorce during the last seventy years can be made, not in terms of a breakdown in marriage relationships, but as resulting from the increased load which marriage has been asked to carry. When the husband and wife no longer find affection and companionship from their marriage relationship, they tend to question the wisdom of attempting to continue in their marriage. When affection is gone, the main reason for the marriage disappears.

Can Husbands Change?

As I have mentioned, I was a typical inexpressive male who happened to meet and marry an expressive girl. Fortunately, she not only wanted to draw me out, but she succeeded. With her help I began to change my behavior. And, because I was a sociologist, I began to make a study of this whole problem of male inexpressiveness. My studies gave me insights into my inability to communicate with the people I truly cared for, and helped me continue to change.

It has been a lengthy process, because people, even sociologists, don't change overnight. But today I think that I can fairly say that my wife and I can discuss anything whatever with each other—our most intimate feelings, things we have done that we are ashamed of, our fears and weaknesses, and of course the pleasure we take in each other's company. Needless to say, for both of us not only our marriage but our whole lives are richer and happier. And of course the benefit has rubbed off on our children, who have already demonstrated they can tell others what is really going on inside them.

I know, thus, from personal experience, that men who have trouble expressing their deeper feelings can change—if they want to. And I believe that most men, when they come to realize how shy about expressing themselves they really are, generally decide they would like to become more open.

We know from the evidence of other cultures that men are not inexpressive by nature. We see men in many Asian and African cultures who pour out their feelings with ease. In our own society we find that Jewish men and men from a southern European background are more expressive—more willing to cry, to laugh joyfully—than are other men of northern European descent. (It is no accident that I myself am from a Nordic background.) A wife, therefore, should not tell herself that it is "the nature of men" to be shy and reserved.

Of course, this doesn't mean that all men can change easily, or even will want to. A wife may eventually find that her husband is quite content to remain as he is. But I firmly believe that most men will *decide on their own* that they want to become more open and frank, once they begin to see themselves as others—especially their families—see them.

For that is one basic problem. The inexpressive male believes that it is unmanly to reveal his feelings. He thinks it is a weakness, a lack of masculinity, to let his feelings out. He, too, may believe that it is "the nature of men" to be inexpressive. He sees himself, therefore, as being "just like everybody else." And of course he is "just like" a lot of his friends—perhaps his father and brothers as well—because they, too, are reserved with other people.

The beginning, then, is for the man to understand that while he may see himself as the standard American male, his family sees him as silent, shy, reserved, untalkative—use whichever term you prefer. And he should understand how painful this can be for the people to whom he means so much. He should understand, for example, that his wife can be hurt when he reaches for her sexually after he has hardly spoken to her all evening; naturally she begins to think that sex is all she means to him.

Our society has played a rather rude trick on American husbands. First, it discourages boys from expressing feelings of love and tenderness. Then, when they marry it expects them to freely communicate their feelings to their wives. They are given an inconsistent set of standards: to be masculine is to be inexpressive, but to be a husband is to be expressive, to have the ability to communicate and express feelings of love and tenderness.

While that is true, it can be self-defeating to blame one's condition on society. A sound principle which underlies many counseling theories is that, regardless of how a person got to be a certain way, a person must accept who he is and begin to make the choices that will enable him to become who he wants to be.

How a Wife Can Help

A wife can help her husband change. First, she must tell herself not to become fatalistic about the situation. A woman grows up in a family with an inexpressive father. Her mother tells her, "That's the way men are." When she marries, she believes that her husband is different. But then time passes, and she concludes her mother was right after all, that men don't reveal themselves the way women do. She resigns herself to living with an inexpressive man. But she shouldn't.

A wife can begin to help her inexpressive husband to realize how much he has shut off his feelings by saying something like, "I'd really be interested to know what's going on at work—you seldom tell me anything about it." (It is amazing, as studies show, how many wives have only the vaguest notion of what their husbands do for a living.) Or she can say, "You've never told me how it was when you were a kid." Of course she shouldn't make her request a challenge or reproach. She must be genuinely interested in knowing about what concerns him—as indeed most wives are.

By opening up an area a man is fairly comfortable with—his youth, his work, his hobby—and then asking him how he felt or feels about it, a wife will find it easier to lead her husband into more open conversations. It may be fairly easy for a man to tell his wife what he does at work; it is going to be much harder for him to say he enjoys his work, or is bored with it, but that is really what is crucial to communication between spouses. Similarly, he may be able to say fairly easily that he used to play football every afternoon after school on the corner lot; it is going to be a lot harder for him to say he felt miserable because he wasn't very good at it, or describe the thrill he got the time he caught a touchdown pass. But again, his feelings are the crucial matter.

I suggest, then, that from time to time a wife try her husband on such straightforward topics. If he shrugs her off with a noncommittal answer—"I don't mind my work"—she might try once more—"But you seem discouraged lately and I wondered if something at work was bothering you." If he remains noncommittal, she's probably best advised not to press him, but to bide her time.

Once a man begins to open up a little, a wife must be encouraging and supportive. This isn't always easy. Suppose she asks him about his job, and suddenly, for the first time, he blurts out that he hates it and wants to quit. Understandably, she may feel a moment of panic, and say, "Oh you can't do that, think of the children," or some other negative reaction. It is far better to say something like, "From what you tell me about it, I don't blame you, I'd hate it too." Few men

will simply quit their jobs and leave their families in
the lurch. By opening the subject up, perhaps with her
encouragement, husband and wife together can find a
happier career for the husband.

The key is for the wife to open her heart when her
husband is offering to share some of his feelings. She
may not always think he is right; she may feel that he
shouldn't have felt so angry when his boss criticized his
work, or when his father gave his brother his old car.
But if she wants him to communicate with her, she
must show sympathy. I don't mean that a wife should
play up to her husband, that she should blindly agree
with everything he says; but it is always wise to temper
the truth with compassion.

The point is that a wife doesn't have to agree with a
husband's viewpoint to sympathize with his feelings.
Suppose a husband has had a disagreement with a
friend or relative—his father, for example. He says
angrily, "I can't get anything through his thick head."
The wife may feel that they're both wrong, perhaps,
but the important thing is for her to support her husband in any case. She can say something like, "I know
you're really angry right now; I wonder what's making
you so mad?" Once she has gotten him to ventilate his
feelings on the subject, it can then be time for her to
say, "I understand what you're feeling, I'm wondering
if you've thought about . . ." This may provide him
with a different viewpoint of the situation which will
help him reach a solution. She may go on, "I want you
to know how much it means to me that you're sharing
this with me. Right now I have mixed feelings about the

situation but I hope it's helpful to talk it out this way."

This is what psychologists call "positive reinforcement." The husband is being rewarded—in this case with his wife's appreciation—for his act, and this inevitably encourages him to repeat it. It may sometimes be difficult for the wife to be supportive of her husband's efforts to be more communicative, especially when he expresses troublesome feelings about his job, family, or other matters that are important to her; but she should try to remember that she can always go over the ground again later. The immediate point is to encourage him to go on talking.

A second, most important thing a wife can do is to assure her husband that she is secure in his masculinity —that she has no doubts about his "maleness." She can do this quite simply by telling him occasionally what a good man he is. She may also encourage him by saying something like "I feel it takes a strong man to show tenderness and be gentle. It makes me secure with you." The surer he feels that she sees him as solidly male, the more he can allow himself the "weakness" of opening up his feeling to her.

Finally, a wife should be expressive herself. There are shy women in this culture, too—although not nearly as many as men. By giving something of her own spirit, by revealing her own feelings, she can go a long way toward encouraging her husband to open up, too.

Being open herself helps in one surprising way. Curiously, a man who doesn't express himself easily sometimes fails simply because he doesn't quite know how. He literally doesn't know what words to use. Those who are used to being expressive find the words roll easily; those who aren't, however, may not be able to find the words at all. There are many ways to say what we feel; but using them sometimes takes getting used to. Thus, when a wife says, "Thanks for cheering me up last night when I needed it," or, "I really feel close to you sometimes like today," or, just, "I love you," she is, in fact, giving her husband a lesson in the expressive forms of the English language.

Change Must Come from Within

I have perhaps made it seem as if it were a wife's job to change her husband, but of course that isn't true. A wife can help. She can give her husband a better picture of his inexpressiveness and how it affects the rest of the family. She may be supportive and encouraging or model expressive behavior herself. But change must come from within the husband.

If any of you recognize yourself in this portrait as the "John Wayne" type of man, you might ask yourself whether you would rather be more open and expressive of your love with your wife than you are now. If you would, you can make a beginning by simply trying to talk more often about what you *really feel*. I know from personal experience that it isn't easy. It was very hard for me at first to begin to tell my wife that I cared for her, to tell her that I loved her, to share my feelings.

But I did it, and the rewards have been enormous. Not only has my marriage been enriched, and my relationships with my children deepened, but the change has spread through my whole life. Because I am willing to let people see who I am in my strengths and weaknesses, I have become a better teacher, a better friend, even a better scholar. For after all, one of the jobs of a sociologist is to learn about people, and how can you ask people to tell you who they are, if you aren't willing to tell them who you are in return?

NOTES

1. W. H. Manville, "The Locker Room Boys," *Cosmopolitan,* 166, no. 11 (1969): 110–15.
2. Alfred Auerback, The Cowboy Syndrome. Summary of research contained in a personal letter from the author, 1970.

4

Why Wives Can't Say
"I Love You"

THE TELEVISION SERIES "All That Glitters" was based upon a plot which completely reversed the stereotypical role of the husband and wife in America. A typical scene in "All That Glitters" would be for Paula to come home from her day's work at the office and ask her husband Bob, "What's for dinner?" Bob would then start complaining about the difficulty of preparing the meal while tending to the needs of their three small children. As Paula proceeds to her favorite easy chair to watch the evening news, Bob hurries around the kitchen and prepares the table for the evening meal.

Later that evening, after Bob has washed the dishes and put the children to bed, he comes over to the sofa where Paula is reading some briefs she will present at the office board meeting the next day. Snuggling up to Paula he asks, "Darling, do you love me?"

Paula pauses from her work, looks at Bob, and while patting him on the head, replies, "Why do you seem to be so unsure of my love, dear?"

Bob replies, "Well, you never ever tell me how you feel about me. I work hard here at home all day long and when we have these few moments to be together at the end of the day, you are absorbed in your office work."

A knowing smile appears on Paula's face, as if to say, Now it's time to give the little husband a little security. Paula pulls Bob closer to her, gives him a hug and says, "Why darling, you know that I love you."

Bob seems only half-assured by Paula's words, as he retorts, "Then why do you tell me that only when I ask you?"

At this Paula begins to get a little impatient with the emotional needs of her husband. Hoping to get back to her work, she replies, "Because you are always asking. You never give me a chance to tell you voluntarily that I love you."

With this Bob runs to his bedroom sobbing, "You never share your feelings with me, you are more interested in your work than in me."

We can watch a television program like this and laugh because it seems so "out of character," quite the opposite of what we experience. It seems very humorous, and even a bit strange for a wife to have more difficulty expressing her feelings than her husband.

While marriage typically is more hindered by the inexpressiveness of the husband, the husband does not necessarily have a corner on the marital inexpressiveness market. There are some societal factors which work against being open and sharing for both wives and husbands. Many of the reasons for inexpressiveness which were discussed in chapter 2 apply to wives as well as husbands. Wives may not express love towards their husbands because of fear, low esteem, embarrassment, lack of time, talking about trivia, and so on. However, in this chapter we shall concentrate only on those reasons for inexpressiveness which are distinctive to the wife's role.

Wives as Social-Emotional Leaders

At first glance it may appear that there are no reasons for inexpressiveness which are distinctive to the role of the wife. This can be illustrated in the way some sociologists have described the leadership differences between husbands and wives. Husbands, they say, are instrumental or task leaders. This involves such activities as seeing that the family has enough food to eat, sufficient clothing and protection from the elements. Wives, on the other hand, are the social-emotional leaders. They provide for the emotional needs of family members and the social relations between them.

If we look deeper into a marriage relationship, however, we will find some reasons why wives may not express their feelings to their husbands. Wives do not say "I love you" to their husbands because they seldom hear it from their husbands.

When Love Is Not Returned

Have you ever wondered why you repeat certain expressions of affection to one person and not to another? Much of how we express ourselves to another is dependent upon how that person responds to us. This is also true in the marriage relationship. To illustrate this let us consider the manner in which three newly married couples might greet each other after a day apart. In all three cases, both husband and wife work, and the spouses get home from their work at about the same time. All three couples started their marriages very much in love, and were very affectionate and considerate towards each other.

The first couple, Ruth and Warren, warmly embrace each other when they are together again after their day at work. Either Ruth or Warren can be expected to say, "It's really good to be home with you, Honey!" The other is likely to respond by saying, "Yes, you're something to come home to!" Both feel free to verbalize their love for each other in a mutually responsive way.

When the second couple, Mary and Ted, get home, they also share a warm embrace. However, it is always Mary who initiates a conversation. She may say, "I missed you, today!" after which Ted can always be counted on to return with "I missed you too," or "Me too."

The third couple, Sue and Gordon, also embrace each other warmly, and Sue says, "Hi, Sweetie, it's good to have you here with me." Instead of any verbal response, Gordon either smiles or gives Sue a squeeze of the hand.

Although the husbands differed in their verbal expressiveness, all of the wives were equally able to initiate verbal affection towards their husbands. It would be interesting to visit each of these couples again in another year or two. How might we expect the nature of their greetings to have changed? In the case of Ruth and Warren, who both freely and mutually expressed affection, both have also experienced the positive reinforcement of having initiated expression and of having affection verbally returned. Chances are that such positive reinforcement would contribute to a continued expressive relationship between them.

What would the conversation between Mary and Ted be like after a year or two? Here Mary was always the initiator and Ted could be counted on to return verbal expressions of affection. The chances are that Mary will continue her verbal expression of affection, because of the positive reinforcement given by Ted. One wonders, however, how long Mary will initiate such greetings when Ted never does.

How about the greeting at the end of the working day for Sue and Gordon? Not only is Sue the initiator of verbal affection, but her expressions are never verbally returned. We may expect that Sue's verbal communication will be greatly diminished after a year or two in which Gordon never so much as utters a single word of affection in return.

When an expression of love is not returned, it is less likely to be offered a second time. Over a period of time, the lack of positive reinforcement may diminish the verbal expression of love completely. Many wives begin by saying "I love you" to their husbands, but through the years come to be like their husbands in not expressing their feelings. But it is also possible that if the wife persists, the husband will become like her and begin to express his feelings.

The Arrival of Children

In our society it is expected that both the husband and the wife will express affection to each other, although the wife may contribute more to a marriage in this regard. But when it comes to child-rearing, mothers are clearly expected to assume the major responsibilities in caring for children. This is especially true when the children are young, when their needs for tender loving care are greatest.

The birth of a child then is an added emotional burden which the mother is asked to carry, and as a result she may decrease her expressive attention to her husband. As the child grows older, she/he is able to provide for some of the emotional needs of the mother. The child becomes an object of the mother's affection and increasingly a source of returning affection also. It may be tempting for a mother to give and express love and attention to the children at the expense of her husband. This may be especially true when her husband has been the one needing expressions of affection rather than the one giving expressions of affection. The comparison between a child who can freely say, "Mommy, I love you," and a husband who is limited to physical means of expressiveness need not even be consciously made by the wife. She, as with all of us, is drawn to persons who are expressing their love to her.

Fear of Vulnerableness

Marriage is a demanding relationship. Spouses are expected to be many things to each other. They learn

to depend upon each other for their needs. It is easy
for one spouse, with sufficient motivation, to take advantage of the other. But, paradoxically, it is the will-
ingness to make oneself vulnerable, to share and open
up to the other, that allows for a close intimate relationship to develop. The wife whose husband has never
opened up may fear taking the first step—it can be a
terrifying prospect. When both husband and wife
openly share their feelings, vulnerability is lessened.
The wife's fear of being vulnerable is not so much
rooted in revealing her feelings, as it is in revealing her
feelings *for* her husband. For a wife to reveal her feelings to a silent, unresponsive husband results in her
feeling vulnerable in her exposure.

Fear of Bargaining Loss

One way to picture a marriage is as an exchange of
goods. Two persons date, size up the different dating
partners and finally "strike a bargain" with the one
they choose to marry. Although the concept of commitment is present in most marriages, the relationship itself can be understood as an ongoing bargaining process.
Both partners will continue in the relationship as long
as they believe they are getting a sufficient amount in
return for what they are putting into it. The "commodity" in marriage can be money, goods, time, help,
love, encouragement, or anything which a spouse values.
When one partner comes to the conclusion that much
is being given but little is being received, then the wisdom of continuing in the relationship is questioned.

In such a view of marriage, the communication of

love can be thought of as a commodity in the bargaining process. If so, then it can be held back and given only in return for what is desired in the relationship. I am not arguing that this is the way marriage necessarily *should* be, but it is the way marriage *may* actually be conceived by the marriage partners.

In a response to some of my theoretical writings on the inexpressive male, another sociologist has raised an interesting point. I have explained male inexpressiveness as a result of the socialization process in American society. He has suggested that male inexpressiveness is a form of sexual politics, that men are inexpressive of their feelings as a conscious attempt to *control* interpersonal situations. If wives perceived that their husbands withheld expressiveness as a conscious effort to control, then they too might be tempted to withhold their expressions of affection as part of the bargaining process. That is, they might come to withhold the giving of affection until their husbands give a little themselves.

Marital Disinterest, Dependence, and Power

Related to the fear of losing bargaining power, is the effect which disinterest on the one hand and overdependence on the other can have upon power in a marriage relationship. Simply stated, the spouse who shows the least interest in the marriage relationship stands to gain power in the relationship, while the spouse who shows an overdependence in the marriage stands to lose power. The spouse who is dependent upon the marriage dare not make too many demands, for fear that the other may want to terminate the relationship. The dis-

interested spouse can fairly well have his or her way,
by being demanding and threatening to leave unless
the other spouse yields. In a marriage relationship of
this type, for the dependent spouse to say "I love you"
to the disinterested spouse would in effect result in a
loss of power. Saying "I love you" could be interpreted
as a sign of dependence. When a disinterested spouse
can take the other spouse's love for granted, then the
spouse who loves is powerless. The wife who finds herself in such a powerless situation might be very tempted
to stop communicating love. A wife may even *pretend*
disinterest in the marriage as an attempt to gain back
some of the power she has lost in the relationship.

Help for the Inexpressive Wife

The foregoing discussion is an explanation as to *why*
wives sometimes cannot or do not express their affection
to their husbands. I have not been advocating ways in
which wives ought to relate to their husbands. I am
committed to the view that free and open verbal expressions of affection between a husband and wife will
result in the greatest growth potential in a marriage
relationship. But in view of these reasons why a wife
may not feel free to express affection to her husband,
what can she do? In the previous chapter I suggested
several ways in which an expressive wife might help her
inexpressive husband to open up. All the suggestions
given there can equally be applied to the inverse situation in which a husband can express his feelings, but
the wife is inexpressive. In such a marriage it is the
husband who must take the lead in talking about his

feelings, in being sensitive to the emotional needs of his wife, and in assuring her of his love. The expressive husband will seek to cultivate a caring, loving, and trusting relationship within which his verbally inexpressive wife will feel free to open up. I believe in complete emotional equality in marriage. The husband is no less responsible for the emotional security and responsiveness of his wife than she is for his.

If it were the case that women and not men had the most difficulty in expressing affection in our society, then I would feel free to rewrite the third chapter and merely invert the words *man* and *woman,* and *husband* and *wife.* It is true, however, that when there is an expressive difference in a marriage, in the vast majority of cases the husband is usually the least expressive.

What help is there for the wife who has become inexpressive towards her husband because the expression of love has not been returned, or because of the fear of vulnerability, or the fear of bargaining loss, or the fear of overdependence?

First, I would stress that there are no easy answers to these questions, even though some have been advocated. Some rather simplistic answers I have categorized in two types, the *aggressive wife syndrome* and the *submissive wife syndrome.*

The aggressive wife syndrome is one that encourages women to demand their fair share by becoming aggressive in the marriage relationship. Advocates of this position argue that the day of the patriarch who demands obedience of his wife is over, and that wives must not tolerate such demonstrations of authoritarianism. This view, supported and sensitized by the women's liberation movement, seeks forcefully to demand women's rights in the home as well as outside the home.

In the *submissive wife syndrome,* the opposite approach is taken. Here the wife is told to submit herself totally to her husband, yielding to every demand that he makes. Such advocates usually argue that God intended for man to be the head of the home, and that woman was created to be his helper. There is a chain of command, it is suggested; all authority is passed down in a neat hierarchy starting from God, who has authority over the husband, who has authority over his wife, who has authority over the children. In such a view the wife is promised that the husband will eventually come around to being the type of husband she desires, if she will only submissively endure with patience.

I have no doubt that the aggressive and submissive wife syndromes do work in many marriages. With both of these easy-answer approaches, there is an ample supply of wives who are more than willing to testify to the glorious change which has resulted in their marriage due to the formula they have followed. One rarely hears testimonies, however, from those women whose marriages did not improve. Many of the marriages where the wife has chosen to become aggressive, have ended in divorce. The divorce rate has dramatically risen during the past eight years, closely corresponding to the rise of the women's movement.

I am not, here, speaking against the women's movement. I am in agreement with the majority of its aims and feel that women need to be liberated from the role of a repressed minority. I am stressing, however, that the immediate effect of wives' increased aggressiveness in the home has often meant at least a short-term disruption and sometimes a permanent disruption in the marriage relationship. Those of us who were brought up valuing traditional dichotomous definitions of masculinity and femininity are having problems adjusting to the more flexible definitions of masculine and feminine behavior. Young people marrying today may not have this problem, because they have been exposed at an earlier age to an androgenous view. Changes as a result of questioning sex role stereotypes will most likely improve the quality of marriages in the future. The difficulty is with people who have grown up and married before the women's movement, and in the 1970s have had to learn new definitions of what a husband's and wife's roles are all about. It is not surprising to find that the greatest increase in the divorce rate has occurred among those couples who have been married for more than ten years.

Although the marriages in which the wife dutifully submits to her husband do not as often end in divorce, they are rarely noted for being growth-engendering relationships. I am fully convinced that a marriage relationship has the greatest chance of becoming intimate *when both* the husband and wife live with an attitude of total submissiveness to the other. It seems that this is what the Apostle Paul had in mind when he said in Ephesians 5:21, "Be subject to one another out of reverence for Christ." I find it rather revealing and more tragic than amusing that most of those who tend to emphasize submission on the part of the wives only, start quoting Paul in the following verse: "Wives, be subject to your husbands, as to the Lord" (v. 22). The verses which follow Ephesians 5:21 can be understood only in terms of Paul's emphasis on *mutual* submission.

I do not wish to get involved at this point in the controversy over authority in the Christian marriage. But it is necessary to examine authority in marriage to the extent that it is related to the problem of verbal expressiveness in marriage. I contend that the traditional view which has emphasized a dominant husband/submissive wife relationship has served to inhibit open and free expressions of feelings in the marriage. To test my contention I would ask you to do three things right now:

(1) Make a list of five of the persons with whom you are most able to share your feelings.

(2) Make a list of five of the persons with whom you have difficulty sharing your feelings.

(3) Analyze the degree to which you consider yourself equal or unequal with the persons on each list. What I think you will find is that you are most free to reveal yourself to those persons with whom you consider yourself most *equal* in terms of authority. The greater the emphasis upon superordinance-subordinance in a relationship, the lesser the degree of emotional sharing that will take place.

As Paul elaborates on the relationship between a husband and a wife in Ephesians 5, he emphasizes love rather than the submissive issue. The motivating force in a marriage relationship must be love. In Eric Segal's novel, *Love Story,* the most remembered line has come to be "Love means never having to say you're sorry." The submissive wife syndrome implies a similar sentiment, "Love means that the wife should never make demands on her husband." I do not agree with either of these statements. People who love each other will do and say things to each other which they are sorry for, and they will need to say, "I'm sorry." Likewise, wives should sometimes make demands on their husbands *because* they love them. And the reverse is true.

When mature love is present between a married couple, they will *both* accept responsibility for the relationship. A large part of accepting responsibility is to make demands—to confront or challenge the other when that person is not upholding their end of the relationship. The wife is as responsible for correcting the husband as the husband is for correcting the wife. There are times when the wife should challenge her husband to become more communicative of his feelings. She is not limited merely to being an example for him. She has a right to demand that he share himself with her as she shares herself with him. Instead of becoming inexpressive herself, the wife needs to be assertive with her husband.

It may be good at this point to distinguish between aggressiveness and assertiveness. Aggressiveness is action which does not respect others' rights—to have your way by putting down the other person. In assertiveness, however, the rights of the other are respected along with one's own rights. Assertiveness is not to put the other down, but to say, "I have rights too."

The wife who is inexpressive because her husband is not what he should be in the marriage relationship must assert her right to be involved in a full, intimate relationship with him. She must resist both the temptation to cop out or give up, and the temptation to submit. She must not come to the conclusion there is nothing she can do to make the relationship better.

5

Why Parents Can't Say
"I Love You"

"Do you really love me?" is the question most grade school children would ask their parents if they were assured they would get a truthful response. This is the finding of family life educator, Dr. Paul Popenoe. Most parents will probably be surprised at this. If anything is taken as a given by most parents, it is that their children know that they love them. However, Dr. Popenoe's findings show that children obviously question their parents' love for them. Why, we ask, are they questioning their parents' love? Could it be the result of insufficient demonstration or verbal expression of parental love?

As parents, we tend to be unaware of our children's need for the expression of the love we take for granted. We recall the many hours of care and training we have given, the sacrifices we have made, and we conclude that our children must be convinced of our love. In other words, we tend to assume that our children will take all that we have done for them as a sign of our love. In the process we have tried to substitute the giving of things for a giving of ourselves. As parents, we are also likely to believe that our love for our children is unconditional and therefore unquestionable. To question our love may actually come as a shock to most parents.

The Importance of Parents' Saying "I Love You"

Shocked or not, the fact remains that children are insecure about their parents' love and have a tremendous need for hearing that they are loved. The receiving of love is vital to a child's physical, social and psychological development. As mentioned in chapter 1, children who do not receive an adequate amount of love while they are infants may literally waste away and die. In less deprived situations, a child may simply fail to develop a healthy self-concept or sense of self-worth and self-esteem.

In the next chapter, I will discuss in detail the importance of the development of a healthy self-concept in a child. It will have to suffice here to say that it is vitally important for us as parents to express love to our children while they are young, because such expressions will be internalized by the children, that is, become part of a child's self-concept and way of living. They will have a snowball effect that continues throughout life. Unfortunately, negative self-concepts also have a snowballing effect which continues throughout life, and are difficult to change. This is a simple but all-important reason why we must clearly communicate love to our children.

Expression of Love Between Parents

An important aspect of parenting which is often overlooked is the need for parents to express their love to one another. Husband/wife relationships are much simpler before children enter the picture. Each spouse bestows affection and love upon the other, and the couple looks to each other as a reciprocal source of affection, love, and support. When a child enters the home, however, family relationships become more complex.

Parenthood is often a time of stress in the marital relationship. Most couples, in fact, find becoming parents to be a more difficult adjustment than becoming married. They have generally become adjusted to each other, but now new changes are demanded in a new family system. Any changes tend to create fear, anxiety and uncertainty, for they involve breaking patterns and making adjustments to new patterns. The couple are taking on new roles as mother and father, with new duties to perform, new demands on their love and time, and new responsibilities to the child.

The ability of spouses to express love to one another during this time of stress is most desirable and necessary. One of the important things a father can do for his infant child is to communicate his love to the child's mother. When she becomes a mother, a wife has an increased need for expressions of love from her husband. She is the primary source of gratification for the infant's rather taxing emotional requirements, but the infant at first is not able to direct positive emotions toward her in return. So she turns to her husband for greater emotional input to enable her to continue to meet the infant's demanding emotional needs and replenish her own spent emotional resources.

A new mother is also likely to feel some insecurity in taking on the tasks of infant care, and so the need for reassurance from her husband in the form of emotional expressiveness increases. Her new motherhood may also attack her self-image as an attractive female. Having just gone through the physically altered state of pregnancy and finding that infant care leaves her much less time and energy to devote to personal beautification, she may strongly desire reassurance from her husband that she is still attractive and loved. A sensitive father will express his love often to his wife and the mother of his children. By promoting her emotional stability and security, he can enable her to relate more effectively to the infant.

The new mother is not the only one, however, who needs expressions of love and reassurance. The new father does too. Before the birth of the first child, the husband is the *sole* object of his wife's attention and affection. After the child is born, he must share this attention and affection with the newcomer. Many husbands are ambivalent about the arrival of a new child but often afraid to admit it. It is a rare husband who doesn't welcome the birth of a child as one of the most cherished events in his life. At the same time, however, it is easy for the husband to experience feelings of resentment over the attention the newborn child demands from his wife, often at his expense. The ambivalent husband may not recognize or understand these feelings, or may even deny feelings of resentment which may be present. A sensitive wife will show her love for her husband at this time, and assure him of his place in her life.

Jointly sharing in the care and training of children can also directly benefit the emotional quality of the marriage relationship in at least two ways: (1) It relieves the mother of the often taxing burden of child-care, thus giving her more time for her own needs as well as giving her energy for the husband/wife relationship. (2) It involves the husband with his children in a meaningful way, thus better enabling him to establish expressive relationships with family members other than his wife.

Parenthood can be a crisis period, when parent's expressive needs are at their maximum. As children grow older, they can become sources of expression of affection to parents. However, children can best learn to be expressive by having parents who are not only expressive to them, but also expressive to each other. Expressing love to *each other* is one of the best gifts parents can give to their children.

How Fathers Differ From Mothers in Expressing Love

Mothers and fathers differ somewhat in the way they emotionally relate to their children. Mothers are probably equally affectionate with their daughters and their sons, sharing hugs, kisses and verbal affection with their children regardless of their sex. Fathers, however, may

be more free to show affection to their daughters than
to their sons. A father views his daughter as one to be
held, hugged and cuddled, and treated in a gentle manner. But to cuddle a son, and treat him in a tender way?
That's something else! Boys need rough-housing. They
need to be taught how to be a man.

Relationships between fathers and sons in our society
tend to be what sociologists call instrumental, that is,
task-oriented, while relationships between fathers and
daughters tend to be expressive. Research has shown
that daughters rather than sons rate their fathers high
in the giving of nurturance and affection. These findings suggest that the inexpressive father may be overly
concerned about masculinity. He is more likely to be
preoccupied with the masculine development of his son,
while encouraging femininity in his daughter and thus
interacting with her in a more expressive way.

The next time you hear a father proudly proclaim,
"That's my boy," or "He's all boy," pay attention to
the context of this pronouncement. Has the son just
given his little sister a big hug, or his mother a big kiss,
or told his brother how much he loves him? Hardly!
The chances are that a father has just witnessed his son
challenge the neighborhood bully, or skin his knee
climbing a tree, or engage in some other type of sufficiently "masculine" behavior. Especially in relating to
their sons, fathers have a difficult time expressing their
love.

The inability to say "I love you" seems to be less a
problem for mothers. Certainly, some mothers are not
as free in expressing their feelings with their children

as they would like to be. But this is more likely a result of their own personal background than it is of their gender.

Inexpressive Parents

Let's take a closer look at the nature of the relationship between parents who have trouble expressing their feelings and their children. As we have seen, motherhood and fatherhood require an increased emotional load, and many parents are not prepared to handle the load. Fathers, especially, but parents in general have not been encouraged to develop the human relation skills necessary to adequately meet the demands for emotional expressiveness which are placed upon them as parents.

Because the mother is the infant's main source of emotional satisfaction, she may be very frustrated by the demands on her at all times of day. At this point, the father is usually expected to develop a comfort-giving relationship with his child and, as mentioned earlier, provide the extra emotional support his wife needs. Ironically, inexpressive parents may feel more comfortable in expressing emotion to their infant child while it is lacking any sort of self-awareness than they will be after the child begins to develop into an individual.

As the infant gains a sense of self-awareness and grows into a child, the parents' expressive tasks continue. Here the father's role includes activities which expand the exhibiting of love in many ways—picking the child up, cuddling him, talking baby talk to him, playing with him. Thus, as the emotionally nondemanding infant grows into a child, the father experiences a corresponding mounting of expressive demands, which continue to expand as the child develops.

The way parents relate to each other sets the standard for the way the entire family relates to each other. This not only includes how parents and children express themselves to each other, but also how siblings interact among themselves. The parents' acceptance and open, free expression of emotions and feelings will foster free and open expression between siblings. Stiff, structured communication between parents, in which conversation is guarded, discourages children from expressing their feelings with each other, with their parents, and with others in general.

Parents and Sons

If the inexpressive father has sons, the demands upon him to be expressive are especially acute in the early years of his association with them. Although sons tend to greatly reduce their expressive demands as they approach adolescence, during their early years they can be almost if not as desirous of tenderness, gentleness and verbal affection as girls. Boys between the ages of two and seven possess self-awareness and are greatly receptive of love from their fathers. Little boys are not yet ashamed to sit in their father's lap, to give them a goodnight kiss, or hug them. The possibility of a continued emotionally intimate relationship between a father and his son depends upon how the father acts during this formative period of a boy's life. A secure father will freely show his affection for his "little man." Nothing, not even the affection from the mother, is as important in the development of an expressive male, as is the giving of tender loving expressions from the father.

The affection which mothers show to their sons diminishes less through time than that shown by fathers. However, society warns her not to be overprotective of her son. She is reminded not to make the child a sissy, or to do anything which would hinder his masculine development. And above all, she must not dominate her son.

There may also be a time when a mother's physical expression to her son is considered taboo. As sons mature, they tend to shun their mothers' kisses, hugs, or attempts at physical affection, especially in public. The mother must learn to resist giving any expressions of affection which might be interpreted as "pampering." This is perhaps especially true of boys during latency (ages 7 to 12). After a son's transition into puberty, the mother can more openly show her affection for her son in a relaxed manner. After the son has shown his ability to be involved in dating relationships, and after his masculine identity is sufficiently secure, he once again can allow for his mother's expressions of affection.

In his relationship with his son the inexpressive father is able to enthusiastically engage in "sports talk," which can involve heated discussions over who is the best basketball, football, or baseball player, or what kind of fishing plug to use to catch the biggest bass; or "car talk," which can involve arguments over which car can make it from zero to sixty the fastest, or which of the latest models is the most stylish. However, gut-level feelings are shared only about such "manly topics." The average father feels uncomfortable when his son offers any verbal expressions of tenderness, or brings up such topics as love or even sex. The inexpressive father would rather express his feelings of tenderness and affection towards his son through wrestling with him (when he is young) or playfully slugging him (when he is older). Much joking and teasing between a father and son can actually be substitutes for expressions of affection. This is not to say that physical exchange of joking and teasing are meaningless modes of expression, but they seem to be rather limited means of communication when they are the *only* way a father expresses his warmth towards his son.

Parents and Daughters

The relationship between parents and daughter is both similar to and different from that with their son. As with the son, the inexpressive father will express his feelings to his daughter largely through teasing and joking. He will also be more able to physically demonstrate his love and affection for his daughter than he will through verbal means. However, the older his daughter becomes, the more uncomfortable he may be in showing his feelings physically. This kind of attitude is exemplified in the film *Rebel Without a Cause*. When the sixteen-year-old heroine (Natalie Wood) kisses her father goodbye, her father, both angered and embarrassed, slaps her for behaving in such a way—she is too old a girl for that, he tells her. Admittedly, the father's anger may have some deeper psychosexual implications, but his embarrassment equally indicates that he is unable to handle either the giving or the receiving of affection from his maturing daughter.

Another example of a father's inability to express himself to his daughter is a scene from "All in the Family." Archie Bunker's daughter Gloria has been dangerously ill. Archie walks into the room and sees her lying apparently unconscious. He begins telling her how much she means to him, how much he loves her. But she has been pretending, and suddenly she sits up and exclaims, "It's so great to hear you say it, Daddy." And Archie, instead of taking his child in his arms, snorts disgustedly and shakes her off.

In this scene Archie Bunker acted as if he had been caught doing something wrong. He thinks it is somehow *wrong* of him to tell his daughter how much he cares for her. But why should anyone feel that it is wrong to say "I love you?" Why should a father feel that he shouldn't congratulate his daughter on her good school report card, or tell his boy how much he cares for him?

The mother/daughter relationship has the potential for a great deal of freedom of expression. In our society it is not improper for a mother to show her feelings and express her emotions to her daughter. A mother, therefore, can model the expressive role to her daughter, as her actions communicate that she has nothing to fear in being expressive. There are also specific areas in which it is natural for a mother to share her feelings, ideas, and experience with her daughter—areas such as menstruation, dating, shopping, cooking, etc. Such sharing keeps the door of conversation open.

There may be some aspect of competition between a mother and a daughter's friends which can cause some break in emotional sharing. There may come a time during her teens when the daughter begins to feel a need for independence from her mother and for increased privacy. A daughter, then, will find her peers more reliable in regard to what's acceptable, while her mother's values are increasingly questioned. In working through this stage, a mother may find it difficult to maintain close emotional ties with her daughter. A mother must realize that her daughter may feel a need to become herself—to become autonomous. This need for emotional distance may introduce a time of real struggle. Once independence has been established, however, the daughter can let down the barriers and again allow the emotional sharing and interaction to take place with her mother. A wise mother will rest secure in her relationship with her daughter and think back with understanding to when she too underwent the same identity struggle.

Structural Barriers to Parental Expressiveness

Parenthood requires increased emotional demands for both mothers and fathers. Fatherhood requires that the inexpressive male carry an increased emotional load for which the socialization process has poorly equipped him. He has been discouraged from developing the internal psychological skills he needs. What we may have, then, is an example of what the anthropologist Ruth Benedict has called a discontinuity in cultural conditioning, where males are trained one way, but then expected to behave differently when they are older.

But there are not only culturally acquired *internal* or psychological constraints upon males which keep them from being expressive fathers, there are also *external* or structural constraints. The relationship between the family and the economy provides one example, and the legal system another.

The fact that the father is usually the main link between the family and the economy means, first, that he will not be around the home very much, because his job generally is performed elsewhere. Hence, he will have much less opportunity to be expressive toward his children, even if he wants to be, because his job greatly reduces the time he can spend with them. He must usually crowd any attempts at expressiveness into a few hours at the end of the work day, when his emotional resources for doing so are probably lowest, or into increasingly busy weekends. He may attempt this telescoping of emotional expressiveness into limited time periods by inventing and improvising shorthand symbols of it, such as bringing gifts home, taking the family on a brief excursion for milkshakes after dinner, playing quick-ending games, making jokes, and telling bedtime stories. Some fathers run the risk of becoming little more than stunt men in the process.

Being the main link between the family and the economy also means that for approximately eight hours a day the father is in an environment which, by stressing rationality and emotional control rather than emotional expression, tends to reinforce his initial tendencies not to be expressive. As mothers increasingly become employed outside of the home, all of this may come to be true of mothers too.

Finally, societal norms regulating ties between the family and the economy regard the father as the main link by stressing the priority of his work role even when that involves hardship for the family. Society makes it more difficult for a father to leave his job and thus remove a basic link between the family and the economy. Society expects a mother to give up her job, should it interfere with her relationship to her children, and if the family can possibly do without the income, but the father is expected to give priority to his job over his role as a parent.

The legal system provides further discouragement of the father's development of expressive relations with his children by playing down the father-child relationship. Fatherhood per se and thus the father-child relationship is not a legally acceptable reason for being deferred from the military draft. Divorce laws express preference for the mother-child relationship at the expense of the father-child relationship by usually giving the mother custody of the children and relegating the father to the position of having to seek legal permission to visit his own children. Fathers can be brought into court for not financially supporting their children, but laws say little about the absence of their emotional support.

Becoming More Expressive Parents

We have seen that parenthood entails a sudden increase in demands made upon a father's usually limited capacities for tenderness, gentleness and verbal affection, and that there are certain structural constraints against expressing these emotions. Although a father's emotional capacities may have been augmented through practice at expressing such feelings toward his wife and young children, they are still probably rather limited. If the inexpressive male continues at his same level of expressiveness or even slightly increases it, he will not be able to properly perform the role of father, and family relationships may consequently suffer.

However, it is possible that a man will learn to increase his capacity for and level of expressiveness, especially if he has adopted this solution earlier in connection with his wife's and young children's expressive demands. Some sociologists describe the father-child relationship as a mutually adaptive one, where the father as well as the child adapts himself to the behavior of the other. One characteristic of infants and children which confronts a father is their open and honest expression of feelings, and this can stimulate further expressiveness on his part. It may be, then, that through interaction with his children, the inexpressive father develops increasingly higher levels of expressiveness, and establishes a relationship in which he is not so reluctant to be tender, gentle and affectionate. To the extent that this occurs, the relationship between father and child will probably be strengthened and be better

able to withstand the later onslaught of the cultural gap
which usually separates older from younger generations.

There is much that a wife can do in encouraging her
husband to become more expressive with the children.
The first thing to do is to attempt to establish an open,
honest and sharing relationship with him. Chapters 3
and 4 contain specific suggestions in regard to this.

An understanding wife can try to open up lines of
communication between her husband and the children.
Because he is so untalkative, she has probably done
most of the communicating with them. When one of the
children comes to them and brings up his problems with
a teacher, or simply wants somebody to talk to, she
has been in the habit of doing the answering. But by
directing the child toward his father, she can give her
husband a chance to open up a little. She can say, "Ask
your father about that—he knows more about it than I
do." Or she can say to the husband, "You probably had
the same thing happen to you—why don't you tell
Johnny how you felt about it?"

Parents who learn to express love to their children
can expect to reap rich dividends. For in expressing
themselves to their children, parents are helping to
create the type of children who can freely express themselves back to their parents as they grow older.

6

Why Children Can't Say
"I Love You"

IT IS DIFFICULT to discuss children's expressiveness apart from parent's expressiveness, since the two are so closely interrelated. Much that was said in the previous chapter is relevant to the topic of this chapter.

Social and behavioral scientists have some understanding of the complexity of human development and the many factors which can potentially affect the personality of children. There is considerable agreement, for example, on the importance of the development of a child's self-concept as a factor affecting children's ability to say "I love you." Parents are extremely important in the development of the child's self-concept.

The Development of Children's Self-Concept

A self-concept is simply the view or image a person has of him/herself. Some people have a very positive image, whereas others hold a very negative self-image. Have you ever wondered why some children have such a low concept of themselves? Why, regardless of what you say, some cling to the idea that they can't possibly accomplish anything worthwhile? Such notions are most directly the result of what parents do and say to their children.

Can you imagine what happens when Johnny hears statements from his parents such as, "Boy, that was a stupid thing you did"; or Cindy hears "Can't you do anything right?" and both hear "What's the matter with you, don't you know any better than that?" What do these comments do for Johnny's self-concept and Cindy's self-esteem? The parents are actually defining the child to him/herself. These statements and attitudes provide the major source of Johnny's personal evaluation of himself.

One of the most consistent findings in the study of juvenile delinquents is that these youths have an amazingly low self-concept. Somewhere in their background they have been labeled, "You're no good," "You are a bad one," "You've got a mean streak in you," "You'll never amount to anything," or "You're lazy and worthless." When these evaluations are communicated to children early in life, it doesn't take long before the children *begin* acting in the very way in which they have been defined by their parents. It is natural for children to use parental evaluations of themselves as their own personal evaluations.

There is a cliché that goes, "Nothing succeeds like success." The reverse is also true, "Nothing fails like failure." There is a self-fulfilling prophecy in these labeling statements, in that an expectation functions to actually bring about the expected behavior. Thus, children who begin viewing themselves as stupid or no good soon begin behaving like children who *are* stupid and no good. Shyness and the inability to communicate feelings develop the same way.

A few years ago, when my daughter Jacque was about five years old, I found myself unknowingly reinforcing a shyness developing in her. When introducing a dinner guest to my family, I proudly introduced my boy Jeff, who stepped forward with a gregarious smile, an extended hand, and a "How do you do." Next I introduced my daughter Jacque, who was typically a little less outgoing than her brother on such occasions. I can remember that I had felt embarrassed in the past about her shyly mumbled greeting. So, on this particular evening I found myself saying, "And this is my daughter Jacque; she is a little shy!" Whammo! All of a sudden it hit me. I realized that I had just defined Jacque to herself as a shy person, and in so doing was only serving to reinforce the shy tendency which she was developing.

Notice *why* I introduced Jacque the way I did. To protect *me* from feeling embarrassment when she didn't respond in the forward manner I thought she should. We parents often unwisely reinforce introverted tendencies in our children out of our own uncomfortableness in the situation. What we do is to set up a self-fulfilling prophecy, and our expectations serve to bring about the very lacks we are afraid of in our children.

Fortunately, self-fulfilling prophecies can operate positively as well as negatively. Positive self-esteem and emotional openness emerge as children believe that their parents view them as lovable and acceptable. Children who hear statements from their parents such as, "I really love you," "That was really a thoughtful thing you did," "I really appreciate you," or "You try hard and do good work," come to view themselves in this light ("I'm loved," "I'm appreciated," "I'm thoughtful," "I'm a good worker"). It is not surprising that when these children attempt to do something or relate to someone else, they do so with a sense of self-confidence and self-assurance.

Possession of a positive self-concept means that one expects to succeed, and the expectation of such success can be what is needed to actually bring about that success. Children are capable of loving themselves and others because they have been recipients of love, and a positive response has been made to them. In truth, persons who believe that they are loving will act lovingly towards others. In acting lovingly toward others, these same persons are likely to be defined as loving by the persons who are the recipients of their love, which again adds to their loving self-concept.

Why Do Sons Differ from Daughters?

One of the themes of this book is that females are more likely to say "I love you" than males. On the basis of the best available scientific evidence, however, there is little reason to believe that this is a "natural" or innate difference between the sexes. Scientific study of young children shows very little difference in the emotional character of boys and girls. (The serious reader who would like to pursue evidence is referred to

Eleanor Maccoby and Carol Jacklin's definitive book, *The Psychology of Sex Differences*.)[1] Differences in emotionality between the sexes increase with age, and seem to correspond to the length of time children have been exposed to a culturally based socialization process.

I have done extensive research on the emotional expressiveness of high school children. There are some interesting differences between high school girls and high school boys in their ability to express their feelings. Whereas girls are more able to express their feelings of love, tenderness, warmth, and affection, boys are more able to express their feelings of anger, hate, rage, and resentment. That is because the former types of emotions are stereotypically thought to be feminine emotions, and girls have learned that it is perfectly all right for them to express these types of feelings. The latter list of emotions are stereotypically held to be the masculine type of feelings.

In trying to identify reasons as to why boys are less expressive of love, tenderness, warmth, and affection than girls, I examined the way children had experienced the expressiveness of their parents. I became particularly interested in the type of parenting which produced a boy who *was* able to express his feelings of love. The one important factor which emotionally expressive high school boys had in common was an expressive father. In fact, when comparing boys and girls who both had highly expressive fathers, there was no difference between the sexes in their ability to express love, tenderness, warmth, and affection. The presence of an expressive mother was not nearly as important as the presence of an expressive father towards the development of a boy's ability to express tender feelings.

Probably the most influential hero in a boy's life is his father. If he never hears his father say, "I love you," if he never feels his father's arm around his shoulder hugging him, if he never sees his father cry, his impression is confirmed that these are things men don't do. Part of the lessening of expressive demands on the part of the adolescent boy may be a result of the inexpressive way in which his father chooses to interact with him. Inevitably, by the time he is a teenager he has learned not to show his feelings of love, tenderness, or affection.

I have been generalizing about the differences in expressiveness between sons and daughters. Certainly there are many brothers who are more expressive than their sisters. However, this is the exception rather than the rule. Daughters are reinforced in a positive way when showing tenderness, crying, and expressing their feelings. Sons, on the other hand, are given negative feedback when they show similar expressions. These expressions are defined as "feminine" qualities and not to be part of a boy's repertoire.

Parents seem especially concerned that their sons conform to the masculine role. This is especially true of fathers who demonstrate grave concern when their son acts "sissy." Even grown men can remember back to the terror they felt whenever they were called a "sissy." This was the epitome of insult to the male role. Sons unfortunately come to avoid verbal expressions of love because of the "sissy" connotations associated with this type of behavior.

Grown Children

Although sons and daughters don't remain children for long, they do remain children to their parents for much of their adult life. The lengthening life span has resulted in an increasing proportion of our population belonging to the senior citizen category. These elderly persons are in need of knowing that they are loved, perhaps even more at this time than at any other time in their life since childhood.

It may be that these elderly parents were not as able to be expressive of their feelings towards their children as they would have liked. As a result, their children are not able to express their love freely in return at the time in their life when it is most needed.

As children become adults, they find themselves more on the caring end of the relationship with their parents. They need to accept the responsibility of communicating love to their parents. But it may be difficult to suddenly begin saying "I love you" after years of relating in an uncommunicative pattern. Both parents and children may be uncomfortable with a more intimate level of communication, even though both may desire it.

Several years ago our family spent our summer vacation in the home of my parents. I always have a longing to come back home, because I have felt a real sense of security there. This is true, even though we were a family which never verbally told each other of our love.

One evening an argument developed between me and my mother. As the argument grew, it became apparent that neither of us was going to convince the other of the rightness of our position. We then ended the argument and each went on to do something else. My mother went to the kitchen sink to wash the dinner dishes. As I watched her and was reflecting on what had just happened, I felt bad about our disagreement. So I went over to the sink, put my arm around her, and said, "I love you, Mom."

It was extremely hard for me to work up the courage to say this. Unbelievably, I cannot remember *ever* having told my mother this before. I was very uncomfortable uttering these words which I felt deeply. My mother, who I am sure cherished hearing these words, was also uncomfortable. Her uncomfortableness was monitored in her reply, "Sometimes I wonder." Unused to a verbal expression of love, she had difficulty responding to it. Since this time, I am glad to report, there has been more freedom between us in expressing our love to each other.

Adult children will find it very difficult to say "I love you" to their parents if they have never done so while living with them. I'm not necessarily advocating that we bombard parents with verbal expressions of our love. However, we may attempt to be sensitive to their needs and think of appropriate situations to show our love.

There are a multitude of ways in which children may communicate their love for their elderly parents. Children who live some distance from their parents can regularly telephone and write letters. The writing of a letter can be an effective way to begin sharing feelings which are difficult to verbalize.

Sometimes it might be possible to make a breakthrough in a relationship. This was the case with my wife Judy, who had always had a comfortable sharing relationship with her mother, but wanted her relationship with her father to be more open. During a Christmas vacation at home with her parents she was able to share her feelings about this with her father. This confrontation continued for several hours in a conversation which was uncomfortable and disturbing to both.

After each spent a restless night, we all had breakfast together the next morning. During the breakfast prayer, Judy's father referred to the previous day's conversation. He prayed that his children might really know of the love he had for them. There was such tenderness in the manner in which he prayed, that Judy was reassured of his love. Later that day we prepared to leave for our long drive back to our home. As we left, her father was able to say, "I do love you, Judy," as they embraced. This proved to be a real breakthrough in their relationship and it has continued to the present time.

One of the fallacies taught in our society is that we are the way we are and we cannot change. We may be tempted to accept this rationalization about our relationships with our parents. We reason that since they are the way they are and I am the way I am, our relationship is the way it is and there is nothing that can be done about it. Change is difficult, that is true. But, relationships can change.

Discomforts certainly will occur as we try to change the nature of the relationship with our parents, but change has many rewards. In any relationship, however, two persons are involved and both must thus be involved in the change. It may very well be that our readiness to change a relationship is not shared by our parents. They may not be ready to change. Perhaps they will never be. We may have to be willing to accept our parents for who they are, as they are. This does not mean, however, that we cannot do all we can to show how much we love and care for them. If it ever came to a matter of *either* telling or demonstrating love, the demonstration of love is by far the most believable. There is much that all of us can do in demonstrating our love for our parents.

The point to be made is that although there will probably not be many drastic changes, there can be a number of smaller steps that can be made in improving the quality of relationship we have with our grown parents. There are times when we must very gently try to establish a more intimate relationship with them. Some of these small steps can be very significant in providing a needed foundation upon which a more open relationship with our parents can be built. The significant change may not be a noticeable increase in verbal expressions of love, but rather a changed quality in the total relationship.

How to Help Your Children Become More Expressive

You may be saying, "We sure blew it! We did not establish an atmosphere of open expressiveness when our children were younger. Now that our children are school-aged, there is nothing we can do!"

It is true that the earlier parents begin to relate intimately, the more likely it is that children will be expressive. But it is never too late to change ourselves. Believing in the possibility of change is the key point once again. We can't change others, but when we change ourselves we are changing the situation which can produce change in another.

The first thing that needs to be said is that some of the lack in communication of feelings between parents and children is the responsibility of the children. Parents who have attempted to keep the channels of communication open between themselves and their children have no absolute assurance that children will reciprocate. Also, parents may make the same efforts of communication and expressiveness toward all of their children, only to see different levels of responsiveness from them. One child may be very free and spontaneous, while the other is quiet and reserved, rarely sharing feelings. Parents must accept the fact that there are differences in children with respect to the way they choose to respond.

It goes without saying that you cannot force another person to express feelings unless that person wants to. Parents must accept each of their children for who they are, including how they choose to express themselves. Failure to do this will most likely alienate children, forcing them to construct isolating walls. Children who are unduly pressured by parents soon come to defend themselves, and in the process become all the more reserved. Parents who push and prod, trying to get an emotional response from their children, are defeated even before they start.

The first step in helping inexpressive children is to

totally accept them for who they are. Parents must not
violate the children's rights to deal with their own emotions as they see fit. The second step is to gain the children's confidence. Parents must prove to their children
that they are trustworthy safeguards for their feelings.
Once confidence is gained, children will feel free to
seek out their parents and to share themselves in their
own special way. The manner of sharing may often not
be as forthright as parents would desire, but parents
must be willing to accept whatever their children offer
as a start.

This is especially true when children are angry or
mad, or when they tell their parents, "I hate you." Instead of countering with the natural reactions of anger
and indignation, which swiftly shut a child up, a wise
parent will say something like, "I know these are very
real feelings you're having toward me right now, and
I'm glad you could let me know how strongly you feel."

While parents have the obligation to prevent their
children from acting on their feelings in ways that will
be destructive to themselves and others, they should not
discourage them from verbally communicating any of
their feelings. Dealing with these feelings in a construc-
tive way will provide children with a model for handling
stressful situations that occur between adults who love
each other. If children find that their parents react
negatively when they openly express feelings like anger
or resentment, they may become less free in expressing
their feelings of love and affection as well.

All along the way, parents should not stop making
efforts to share themselves emotionally with their chil-

dren. Such sharing can be in little ways—expressing feelings of being hurt about a comment, angry about an action, sorrow about the loss of a friend, or joy about a gift received. For example, you might have gotten upset during the day, and ended the day by lashing out against your children. Later that evening you might say, "I'm sorry I took my anger out on you, I really was feeling disappointed in myself at work today." In doing this you are showing your children that you're willing to be human and vulnerable to them. This may provide the encouragement for your children to take the risk of sharing their feelings with you.

One caution, however. When you do share your feelings with your children it should not be with the expectation, either verbalized or unexpressed, that "Since I've shared, you should share in return." This sort of expectation, even though it may not be verbalized, puts false and unneeded pressure on your children.

Another way to encourage sharing from your children is to make yourself available to them at appropriate times. Although being available doesn't mean intruding into your children's affairs, it does mean being sensitive to their needs. It means picking up clues as to their desire and need to share, and really listening to them when they do share with you. It is amazing how often parents do not really listen attentively to what their children say. Children are very sensitive to parental inattentiveness. They quickly sense when parents are only pretending to be interested in their comments. When children sense that parents are half-heartedly listening out of a sense of parental duty, they will soon

discontinue sharing themselves. You should be critically
aware of your listening habits with your children. You,
too, may be unknowingly communicating a disinterest
in what they have to say.

I recently observed my wife picking up on a "hidden"
feeling which our daughter was expressing. In anticipa-
tion of the coming school year, Jacque commented,
"Gee, Mom, Jeff would be in my school this year and
I'd be showing him all the ropes." Jeff died of cancer
two years ago, and Judy was sensitive to what feelings
might be contained in this comment. She zeroed in on
the possible hidden feeling by replying, "It makes you
feel kind of cheated out of a special role in his life."
Judy's picking up on the feeling didn't mean that she
was creating an opportunity in which all of Jacque's
emotions about Jeff's death would be expressed. Rather,
her comment served to reinforce the fact that she could
be trusted, and that she understood the deeper feeling
which was present as Jacque verbalized a consequence
which resulted from her brother's death. The next time
it will be easier for Jacque to express another emotion
and perhaps to verbalize it even more openly.

Increasing Intimacy through Family Games

There are a number of "games" which families can
"play" as a means of facilitating the exchange of feelings. I will describe just two such games which my
family found helpful.

In one game, each family member writes on a sheet
of paper the two things they like most and the two
things they dislike most about each other member of

the family. Both Jacque and Jeff wrote that one of the things they disliked most about me was that I teased them too much. As part of the game, they were both able to talk to me about what they didn't like about my teasing and the way it made them feel. This resulted in my becoming aware of my excesses in this area and allowed me to adjust the way I related to them.

Another game is family sculpturing (adapted from Virginia Satir). In this game, all family members place themselves in a desired position in relationship to each other. The game begins with the mother and father arranging themselves in relation to each other. Next the oldest child is invited to find his or her place in relation to the parents without rearranging their postures. Then the next oldest child is asked to do the same, until all members of the family have become a part of the sculpture. After the initial arrangement, other family members get a chance to indicate whether or not they feel comfortable with the arrangement and to suggest how they would like the sculpture to be changed.

When my family did this exercise, Judy and I began by standing in a face-to-face embrace. When Jacque was asked to join the sculpture, she edged in between us so that she was in the center between us. When it was Jeff's turn to join the sculpture, he knelt on the floor and put his arms around the three of us. We then proceeded to rearrange ourselves in relation to each other member. We ended up by having a family sculpture which consisted of the four of us standing in a circle with our arms around each other.

After our sculpturing session, we sat down and discussed the reasons why we felt comfortable with certain formations and uncomfortable with others. For example, when Jeff first joined the sculpture, Judy, Jacque and myself all expressed a degree of discomfort with his kneeling on the floor. We wanted him on our level. He then had to decide if he was ready to be at that level with us. The game and discussion provided insight for all of us.

By means of simple family games such as these, it is possible to facilitate the sharing of feelings between family members which do not ordinarily come about. Parents will find that children are enthusiastic participants. The games give children the opportunity to say something through their action without overdue emphasis on verbal interaction. The ultimate effect of playing family games can be to enable family members to more freely share feelings with each other about their daily life together.

A Personal Note

I was privileged to have a son for ten years who was warm, loving and expressive of his feelings. Jeff died a few days short of his tenth birthday after a three-month fight with cancer. My warmest memories of Jeff center around the times when we were intimate with each other. A bedtime ritual which I established with him was to tuck him in bed and before turning the light out to tell him that I loved him. He would invariably reply, "I love you, too, Dad." Sometimes he even beat me to the punch and would say, "I love you, Dad" before I had a chance to express my love to him.

If any circumstance can be found for making the dying of my son more bearable, it was that I knew his heart. Because of Jeff's openness I knew that he knew that I loved him, and I knew that he loved me and that he loved Jesus as his personal Lord and Savior. The comfort came in being able to hear his expression of love.

We often erroneously believe that to die like a man is to die without showing any feelings. Jeff died like a man, not because he did not show his feelings, but because he expressed them. One evening, lying on the sofa in the living room which had been his bed for a month, Jeff suddenly said to Judy, "Mom, I'm going to die! Mom, I'm going to die!"

When I heard this I came to sit next to him, too. "Dad," he said to me, "I'm going to die! I'm going to die!"

"I know Jeff," Judy said, "is that O.K.?"

"How long will it take?" Jeff asked.

Did he mean until he died or until he got to heaven? we asked, since throughout the illness Jeff was very much aware of his closeness to God and totally secure in the love of Jesus Christ as his Savior.

"To heaven," he answered.

I then assured him that when he died he would immediately be with God. We sensed that this would be the last evening we would share together as a family. That night Jeff died peacefully in his sleep.

A few days after Jeff's death, we were cleaning out the drawers to his dresser and found a note he had written to us sometime in the past. The note read, "I love you, Mom and Dad, even when you get mad at me. I will always love you."

I am grateful to God for having given me a boy who could say, "Dad, I love you."

NOTES

1. Eleanor E. Maccoby and Carol N. Jacklin, *The Psychology of Sex Differences* (Stanford: University Press, 1974).

7

Why Friends of the
Same Sex Can't Say
"I Love You"

A faithful friend is a secure shelter;
whoever finds one has found a treasure.
A faithful friend is beyond price;
his worth is more than money can buy.
Ecclesiaticus 6:14–15 (NEB)

MANY OF THE closest relationships we have are with
people to whom we are not related—our friends. Web-
ster defines a friend as one with whom we are on intimate and affectionate terms. It is true of course that
family members can be friends. One of the joys in life
is that friendships are not ruled out by family boundaries.

Love is very much involved in friendship. Christ
said to his disciples: "This is my commandment, that
you love one another as I have loved you. Greater love
has no man than this, that a man lay down his life for
his friends. You are my friends if you do what I command you. No longer do I call you servants, for the

servant does not know what his master is doing; but I have called you friends . . ." (John 15:12–15).

Friends are persons who love each other and who are willing to give themselves to each other. There is a simplistic saying that goes, "I have no choice about my relatives, but I can choose my friends." There is a certain truth to this, as friendships are based upon choice. A friendship is a relationship between two people who have chosen it to be so. This is part of what makes friendship so special.

Barriers to Friendship

The expression of love between friends is often as difficult as that which occurs between family members. It is particularly complicated in friendships with a married person of the opposite sex. There is often a fear which centers around the potential of romantic and/or sexual involvement accompanying the friendship. I will be talking about the expression of love between friends of the opposite sex in the next chapter. In this chapter I will deal with friendships between members of the same sex. Although this relationship may be less complicated than opposite sex friendships, it, too, is often plagued by barriers which inhibit the expression of love. The two major barriers to intimacy between persons of the same sex are homophobia and competition.

HOMOPHOBIA

Homophobia is the fear of being close to a person of the same sex. As a society we show many signs of this fear, which is connected to the stigma of being branded homosexual or having homosexual tendencies. A college friend of my wife shared the difficulty she was having because of growing affection toward her roommate in the dorm. She questioned her feelings of affection, wondering if she had something wrong with her. Several years later, happily married with two children, she could be more objective about her concern when she came in touch with her affection for another woman.

Psychiatrists claim that the more secure one is in his or her sexuality, the more open one can be in relating to a member of the same sex. The more secure a woman is in her own femininity, the freer she can be in tenderly embracing or verbally expressing affection to another woman. The man who is secure in his own masculinity can put his arms around another man or verbally express his affection to him.

Americans may be homophobic in regard not only to expressing affection to a friend of the same sex but also to touching a member of the same sex. It has been noted by psychologists that most people are "skin hungry." Our society has certain inhibitions concerning touch which often deny people's need to be physically stroked and held. This is illustrated in the conversation between two male friends in James Kirkwood's play, *P.S. Your Cat Is Dead!*

One evening about three months into our friendship, after we'd taken our dates home, we stopped by a bar for a nightcap. We ended up having three or four and when we left and were walking down the street, Pete suddenly slipped his arm around my shoulder. He surprised me;

there was extreme warmth and intimacy about the gesture. When I looked over at him, he grinned and said, "That bother you?" "No . . ." I shrugged in return. He then gave my shoulder a squeeze. "Ever since I've known you, you got me pretending I don't have arms." [1]

Compared to other cultures of the world, American males are very undemonstrative and inhibited about showing love to someone of the same sex. In many cultures of the world, open touching between two male friends is an expression of affection which does *not* have homosexual overtones.

Our family spent a year in the country of Cyprus where I was studying the Greek Cypriot family. There I had the opportunity to observe the relationship between male friends of another culture. One of the intriguing things I noticed was the ease with which Greek males expressed their affection for each other. They not only danced with each other, but were openly free to tell each other what they were feeling. This contrasts sharply with the way American males usually disguise their feelings of affection for each other.

A few years later when studying and traveling in India, I became very close to an Indian man who was my companion for the entire summer. One afternoon we were traveling by public bus to New Delhi and were engaged in deep conversation. Suddenly I realized that my friend Rajgopal was holding my hand as we were talking. I began to feel very embarrassed until I looked around and remembered where I was. No one else on the bus was staring at us in disbelief. No one felt we were doing something wrong by touching each other.

No one suggested there was anything unusual about this physical expression. Here in India it was quite acceptable and often expected that male friends would hold hands or put their arms around each other when they talked.

COMPETITION

Competition is also a barrier to the expression of love between same sex friends. From the time children are born, they are indirectly taught to compete against other members of their own sex.

Females experience competition most in their teenage and premarriage years. They compete in gaining the attention of others, especially boys, using clothes and makeup to accentuate their attractiveness. They learn from a very early age to compare their attractiveness with that of the other girls, and thus the competition creeps in, almost unnoticed. By the time a girl reaches her teenage years, she has learned that although her best friends are other girls, when it comes to attracting boys, they are competitors.

A telling sign of female competition is the unwritten rule that any planned activity with another girl may be broken if a boy is available. When a girl is asked out by a boy, she usually will not let a previous commitment to a girl stand in the way of accepting the date. This lack of loyalty to the girlfriend is taken lightly, as it is assumed she will surely understand the broken commitment. Needless to say, if a girl has a date with a boy and is then asked to join in an activity with a girlfriend for the same time, breaking the date is unthinkable.

Competition for boys serves to foster a sense of tentativeness in relationships between girls. Close friendships between two girls may be developed but are not to interfere with a potential budding relationship of either girl with a boy. This competitiveness serves to foster a basic distrust between girls. They are able to physically express their affection to each other through hugs or embraces, but may hold back their verbal expressions for fear of being vulnerable. At this point in a girl's life, her mother is more likely to be a confidante, because she is usually regarded as a "safe" person rather than a competitor.

Competition between males is of a different sort than that between females. Men do compete for women, but this is part of a wider male competition for success, status, and the need to be looked up to. In the attempt to achieve status, the other man is also a potential competitor.

The more traditional symbols of status are such things as achievements in sports, occupation, education, and the amount of money earned. Men, however, can compete at almost anything, and will do so in order to gain status. In his book *Male Chauvinism! How it Works*,[2] Michael Korda relates how illicit sex becomes a status symbol in the corporate business world. In the seemingly sedate towers of the university, persons often compete fiercely for status with such things as the number of professional publications, or the number of important lectureships one is invited to give. Some professors will not share important scientific information with their colleagues, for fear that someone else will

beat them in publishing the information. Where everyone has the Ph.D., an additional means must be found
to establish a pecking order. Even in a prison, where
all standards of status are stripped away, status may
depend on being the best at playing cards or eating the
most food.

Another rather humorous example of competition is
a personal one which rather ironically shows how far
competition can go. Several years ago, I participated
in a sensitivity group. We were all encouraged to
openly share our thoughts and feelings with the group.
I can remember getting caught up in the competitive
spirit as other group members shared themselves. When
my turn came to share, I was determined to "outshare"
everyone else.

My greatest competitor in this group turned out to
be Doug, an athletic coach who, like myself, normally
had trouble expressing his feelings to others. But when
the name of the game was to share, our inhibitions suddenly evaporated in the promised glory of outsharing
everyone else. After the session, Doug and I had a long
talk about our involvement in the group and examined
the extent to which competition was the motivating
force for our involvement. This helped us gain a better
understanding of ourselves as competitors and the effects it was having on our lives, both positive and negative.

Competition seems to cause barriers. There is a fear
that once one's guard is let down, the other will take
advantage. This guard is, in fact, the barrier which
hinders the establishment of intimacy.

Male Friendships

Although homophobia and competition are barriers which hinder the development of open sharing relationships between men, they do not prevent the development of meaningful male friendships. The type of friendships which men develop with each other is a reflection of the nature of these barriers, however. Let's examine more closely the nature of male friendships by considering two types of men, the *Good Ol' Boy* and the *Locker Room Boy*.

THE GOOD OL' BOY

The good ol' boy is the type of man who has warm and often deep feelings for other men, but he is unable to communicate these feelings verbally. The term *good ol' boy* is primarily a southern expression which has recently been popularized by the mass media's interest in President Carter's brother, Billy Carter. Billy and his male friends who sit in the service station drinking beer and swapping stories are good ol' boys to each other. Good ol' boy relationships do not arise overnight; rather, they are often cultivated during childhood and nurtured through the trials and triumphs of growing up together. The good ol' boy is completely loyal to the other good ol' boys, and together they form a strong in-group or primary group. A good ol' boy is one who can especially be counted on during a time of trouble or need. He is one who you will stick with you "through thick and through thin."

Although good ol' boys spend much time talking to

each other, this talk rarely involves communicating their personal feelings. If asked why he doesn't talk about his feelings, the good ol' boy is likely to reply that it isn't necessary. He may further elaborate, "Man, if you have to say it, the feelings must not be there." He believes that the expression of feelings is a womanly trait. The man who is overly expressive of his feelings is likely to be laughed at and joked about by the good ol' boys as one who is "too sissy" or "too feminine," or who lacks "manliness."

All of this is not to suggest that good ol' boys do not have feelings for each other. They have deep feelings for each other which are enduring and shown in positive concrete *action* which they will take on behalf of each other.

I really believe that most men are good ol' boys to a certain extent. Good ol' boy types of behavior transcend most social, class, geographical, and social boundaries. Every time men go with the guys to a ballgame, to hunt or fish, they are likely to engage in good ol' boy type of behavior.

THE LOCKER ROOM BOY

The locker room boy is similar to the good ol' boy in that he has warm feelings for other men, but he is different because, in addition, he *can* verbally communicate these feelings—but only in the masculine security of the locker room. He is dependent upon such masculine subcultures as men's athletic clubs, sport teams, bars, and gaming rooms. In such environments, where masculine identity is secure, the locker room boy is better able to express his gentler feelings and even demonstrate his affection physically.

Examples of locker room boy behavior transcend social boundaries. After a few beers at the neighborhood tavern, men who have spent the day working in a factory will begin to share their feelings and concerns with each other—emotional sharing which does not take place between them and their wives. Football players will enthusiastically embrace and hug each other following the scoring of a touchdown. In the locker room they will openly weep following defeat, or express affection or love for each other following a victory. Following one of the 1976 World Series baseball games, the New York Yankee fiery manager, Billy Martin, announced to the media that he *loved* his ball players. Since the athlete's masculinity has been established through his physical prowess, he is free to be expressive of his feelings without having anyone, himself included, question his masculinity. The locker room boy is both more comfortable and also more able to share his feelings with certain other men in sufficiently masculine environments.

Liberating Men

Men need to be liberated from the emotional hangups which prevent them from becoming close to other men. How can men learn to express themselves with other men? It may be that the husband who has learned to express himself to his family may be able to extend this expressiveness to include other people.

Another source of change is emerging with the development of men's consciousness raising groups. In a number of communities across the country, men are meeting in small ongoing groups to discuss masculinity and the male role. Many men report that such male consciousness raising groups have been an important source of change for them. Since one of the basic purposes of these groups is to examine man-to-man relationships, it has been found that most men are hungry for the chance to form close personal relationships with other men.

Men's groups can be an effective way for men to gain an understanding about their masculine hangups. They can also provide an impetus to begin to behave differently by creating a climate for the sharing of feelings. Barriers to expressiveness are decreased as men come to experience warmth and acceptance from other men, and see other men revealing a bit of themselves.

An additional benefit, significantly enough, is that the self-disclosure which is generated in these groups seems to carry over in the lives of the men when they return home. One participant in such a group said, "I have never even told my wife about the feelings I have often had. Now, I cannot wait to get home and tell her. What a relief this is for me."

I would hasten to add, however, that such groups are certainly no panacea for the difficulty men have in relating to other men. The groups are highly selective, attracting only those men who already want to find out more about their own masculinity. Further, some men overcome the barriers to male intimacy within the security of the group, but are unable to risk becoming close to men in the real world.

Basically, I would suggest that men who are discontented with the degree of intimacy they have been able to establish with other men should strive for greater intimacy first with those men with whom they feel the most comfortable. Most men already share intimately in some form with others, but perhaps only at select periods of time or in certain situations (locker room boy). The first step would be to expand male intimacy outside of the locker room.

For example, your friend may be talking to you about the upcoming football season and wondering which players will be dropped from your favorite professional football team. You could very naturally interject, "I wonder how a player feels when he is cut from the team?" If your friend picks up on this by suggesting that such feelings as being let-down and questioning personal worth probably accompany such an event, you might reply, "I sometimes wonder how I would feel if I were fired—if my company told me they couldn't use my services any more!" The point is to transcend talking with your friend on a mere superficial level and to begin sharing personal feelings. If you become aware of your conversations with other men, you will find how often you may be just at the edge of communicating emotional feelings.

Female Friendships

There seem to be fewer barriers to intimacy between females than between males. Women seem quite able

to enter intimate sharing relationships with each other.
I would be hard put to come up with a description of a
"Good Ol' Girl" or "Parlor Room Girl," for intimacy
between females does not seem to be restricted to such
situational events.

Some may argue that greater female expressiveness
is a myth. My own judgment is based on the following
considerations. A large number of studies have found
that females disclose themselves much more than do
males. This includes self-disclosing more on the most
intimate of topics. Research shows that women are disclosed *to* more than are men. That is, regardless of who
is doing the disclosing—man or woman—the person
disclosed to is likely to be a woman. All of the evidence
which has been accumulated on self-disclosure leads us
to believe that women share themselves more freely
than do men.

My own research on expressiveness of feelings gives
further support to the view that women are better able
to enter into intimate relationships than are men. They
are able to verbally express their feelings of love, tenderness, warmth, affection, joy, elation, happiness, de-
light, sadness, blues, sorrow, and grief. These are
feelings which one would expect persons in an intimate
relationship to be able to share with one another.

The permission society grants to women to be expressive of their feelings and emotions has afforded
them great advantage in self-disclosure and sharing at
intimate levels. The models and training involved in
child and family caring roles have encouraged women's
skills in human relating, such as attending to others,

listening, empathizing, problem solving, and so forth. It is a benefit which has enriched their lives.

Even though women have often felt the entrapment of the home and routines of housewifery, they have often searched out same-sex friendships and increased intimacy in relationships over a cup of coffee with a neighbor, sharing both the joys and frustrations of being a wife and a mother. Even when housewives are involved in volunteer work outside the home, the work is likely to be socially and emotionally laden. Volunteer work with schools, churches, hospitals, clubs, and fund-raising organizations involve close interaction with others—working with people in "helping" skills, organizing social events, and so forth. The volunteer's socioemotional dimensions are constantly being tapped and developed.

Liberating Women

Whereas men need to be liberated from a masculinity which discourages the expression of emotions and feelings, women need to be liberated from suppressive conditions in our society so that they may have equal opportunity with men to pursue other options than those previously defined as ideal for them. During the 1970s, women have increasingly gained equal opportunities. However, these increased opportunities may be accompanied by an emotional cost.

A natural reaction on the part of women who have gained positions of power and influence in a "man's world," especially those in professional positions, is to take on the competitive, rational, and nonemotional qualities of the business world. The professional woman feels the pressure to prove that she is doing just as good a job as a man. The woman doctor, lawyer, or business-woman may perceive that her male colleagues are just waiting for her "womanly emotionalism" to interfere with her professional competence. A tempting reaction is to be the superrational woman—not letting any emotions show through—and to be more competitive than the males she works with.

When women work outside the home, they are taking on roles which are defined in terms of competence, efficiency, and rational decision-making. The expectations in these work roles are different from the expectations in the home where a wife and mother is expected to be warm, affectionate, gentle, and nuturant.

The point is that the roles which we play in society can, in part, come to shape our behavior. I really believe that one of the main reasons men are less expressive than women is that they devote so much of their time to their work role which discourages emotional sharing. Men learn to relate to other men at work where their roles are task oriented rather than socially or emotion-ally oriented. Women learn to relate to other women around the home where their roles are focused around family relationships.

Women have also found encouragement in sharing and support group activities. In such groups women discuss the challenge of putting together their many roles as woman, wife, mother and worker. As they talk about how to run a household, how to find employment, how to gain ego strength from insecurities about abilities, and how to remain sane while functioning in all areas of life, women are coming to establish close bonds among themselves.

We have considered some of the barriers to close friendships between people of the same sex, and possible ways of penetrating those barriers. Although such friendships may seem uncomplicated, they are often not developed because they are taken for granted. In the next chapter we will turn to friendships that are not taken for granted, but may be more complicated— friendships between people of the opposite sex.

NOTES

1. James Kirkwood, *P.S. Your Cat Is Dead!* (New York: Warner Publications, 1973), p. 23.

2. Michael Korda, *Male Chauvinism: How It Works* (New York: Random House, 1973).

8

Why Friends of the
Opposite Sex Can't Say
"I Love You"

How many women can say, "Some of my most intimate friends are men." How many men can say, "Some of my most intimate friends are women." Probably very few. Opposite sex friendships seem to be most difficult to cultivate and maintain. The tendency is for an emerging friendship to develop into a romantic or sexual relationship, or to stay in stagnation resulting from a fear of illegitimate intimacy.

In a certain sense, any relationship between two members of the opposite sex is a sexual relationship—be it between mother and son, father and daughter, or sister and brother. Our sexual identity is a part of who we are. We can't divorce ourselves from it, and therefore any relationship includes our sexual selves. The fact that this is so has caused us to be very fearful of any close nonmarital friendships with members of the opposite sex, and has caused most adults not to have close and meaningful relationships with members of the opposite sex. It is a rare person who feels the freedom to describe a friendship with someone of the opposite sex as an intimate friendship.

How great a danger is there that an opposite sex friendship will lead to romantic or sexual involvement? This, of course, depends upon a number of factors, not the least of which is the nature of a person's marital relationship. In general, husbands who become sexually involved outside of marriage do so for slightly different reasons than wives. Husbands are less likely to be emotionally involved with the women they have affairs with. Their extramarital sexual involvement is most likely to be merely for the purpose of sexual gratification. Wives who become sexually involved outside of marriage do so more for emotional fulfillment than for sexual gratification.

Intimacy with someone of the opposite sex is potentially explosive. Our sexual orientation and identity influences how we relate to those of the opposite sex. When an attractive man and an attractive woman become close friends, it can be expected that sexual feelings will begin to emerge. Most people handle the potential of opposite sex entanglement by avoidance. Prohibiting closeness between members of the opposite sex is the easy solution. It is much more difficult to establish a basis for legitimate opposite sex friendships. Before we examine this basis for opposite sex friendship, let's consider avoidance as an attempted solution.

Avoidance

Mark and Sue Irwin are in their thirties, are fairly well-adjusted in their marriage, and have three elemen-

tary school age children. Bill and Ellen Jordon are
neighbors who live down the block. They are also in
their thirties, have two children, and their marriage is
basically sound, with only the typical types of disagree-
ments. Ever since Mark and Sue invited the Jordons
over for a backyard barbeque nearly six months ago,
their families have seemed to hit it off together. They
have been to each other's homes numerous times, and
recently returned from vacationing together at the
beach.

The families get along beautifully together, with the
usual amount of teasing that goes on between family
members. This was especially true between Sue and
Bill, as both were big teases. Mark, although good-
natured, was a more serious type than Bill. While Sue
is deeply in love with her husband Mark, she had to
admit to herself that she really liked the way Bill teased
her, and his enthusiastic approach to life. She, in fact,
found herself quite attracted to Bill and flirtatiously
seeking out his attention. She believed that he might
be attracted to her also. Both Sue's feelings and flirtatious behavior began to bother her, make her feel
guilty and frightened. Could she be falling in love with
another man? She was sure of her love for Mark, and
she did not understand the attraction she was having
for Bill.

One day Mark suggested to Sue that they ask Bill
and Ellen to go with them to a movie. Sue surprised
herself when she suggested that maybe they should get
to know Steve and Julie Anderson more, and should
ask them instead. From this point on, the Irwins and

Jordons saw less and less of each other, since Sue usually found some excuse why they could not be together. She never did talk to her husband Mark about her attraction for Bill, and she most certainly did not discuss the situation with Bill and Ellen. She handled her attraction for Bill by simply avoiding contact with him.

Such avoidance is one way out of a dilemma, but it also unfortunately involves a cost. In this case, it cost the Irwins and Jordons a potentially close relationship with each other. Suppose the same thing were to occur in Mark and Sue's relationship with Steve and Julie? Has Sue established a pattern whereby, when she feels confusion and guilt, she will just avoid the situation producing that confusion? Is she developing a pattern of not sharing those feelings with anyone?

Avoidance or withdrawal is a common way for many people to escape from a conflict or solve a potential conflict situation, and it is usually accompanied by a tendency to not share the conflict or problem with another person. It is interesting that some cultures use avoidance as a way of preventing the possibility of close friendships between members of the opposite sex. In the Near East, Muslim societies traditionally have allowed no opposite sex friendships outside of the immediate family. A man could expect to be close only to his mother, his sister, and his wife. A woman could expect to have no friendships with men except her father, her brother, and her husband. The whole reason behind the veiling of women was the prevention of any non-familial intimacy between men and women. Women were thought to have an almost irresistible power over

men because of their sexuality. Men were thought to
be rendered powerless over their sexual urges in the
presence of a woman who did not hide her sexuality—
her legs, arms, and face. Muslims believe that *fitna*
or chaos would result in society if women and men were
allowed the freedom to mix socially in public.

The solution then is avoidance, so that no public
contact is allowed between males and females. Muslim
societies even differentiate space by sex. There is male
space and female space. Any public area—the market-
place, roads, squares, and sidewalks—is male space. A
female is forbidden to enter male space alone; she must
either be with a group of women or be escorted by her
husband, father, or brother. Private space is female
space, and is usually defined within the walls of a home.
Males are not allowed to enter this female space unless
a father, husband or brother is present.

There are very few extramarital physical exchanges
between adult men and women in most Muslim societies.
But, needless to say, there are also very few close opposite sex relationships in these societies. By contrast, in
the United States there is ample opportunity for opposite sex friendships, so much so that some would argue that this has been a cause of many problems in our
society. However, I hold to the ideal that close opposite
sex friendships are both possible and desirable. The
question is, how can these friendships be established?

Establishing Opposite Sex Friendships

Ronda is a counselor working for the Forest City
counseling center. She is happily married to her husband Ben and they have three children. Brent also

works at the counseling center, and he and Ronda often do cotherapy counseling. Brent has been happily married to his wife Nancy for eight years. Although Ronda and Brent are not married to each other, and both are committed to their spouses, they spend much time together at the center and have grown very close to each other. They enjoy working together, appreciate the intellectual stimulation of each other, and find each other physically attractive.

The above fictitious example is similar to the situation in which many men and women are finding themselves. Women today make up over one third of the labor force, and the contact between opposite sex married persons is greater than it has ever been. An increasing reason for divorce in the United States is one spouse's wanting out of the marriage so he or she can marry someone else. One very obvious solution to this problem is not to allow oneself to become close to members of the opposite sex. But this solution rejects any emotional content in a relationship, and the cost is that some very meaningful and potentially wholesome relationships are prevented from developing.

An alternative to closing off growth in relationships with members of the opposite sex is to follow certain principles and guidelines in such relationships. An excellent paper has recently been written by two counselors who describe how they maintained a close professional friendship while also being married to someone else. Sheila Kessler and Jack Clarke have coined the term *createmates* to describe their relationship. In this relationship "there is faith and commitment to the process of the relationship as long as it works. This process has no barriers but it does have limits. There is psychological and emotional intimacy but no physical intimacy." Much of the discussion which follows is based upon the insights of these two.[1]

There are several levels on which a relationship between a man and a woman can operate. In the marriage relationship the husband and wife share themselves with each other on every level—intellectual, emotional, physical. The possibility of a close opposite sex friendship is possible when the following principles are practiced: First, the relationship will involve intellectual, emotional, and psychological intimacy, but not physical intimacy. Second, commitment will be given to the relationship as long as it remains nonthreatening and secondary to the primary marital relationship of each spouse.

PHYSICAL LEVEL

The physical level of a friendship between a man and a woman hungers for sexual fulfillment. It is at this point that many legitimate relationships can be threatened. Upon experiencing sexual attraction and desire for a friend of the opposite sex, our first reaction is often to deny the feelings, because of the guilt and confusion they cause. Denial of feelings, however, is no solution, and ultimately can only have harmful consequences, to ourselves, to our relationship with our friend, and to our relationship with our spouse. I believe that there are very few close opposite sex friendships in which each of us do not at least occasionally have physical feelings. When this occurs, the first thing we must do is to admit the feelings and be openly aware of what is happening. The feelings themselves are not the problem, but rather how one decides to handle them. They can be contained or acted on.

What is the best way to contain sexual feelings in a friendship? First, we should verbalize our feelings, to ourselves, to our friend, and to our spouse. Doing this releases any sense of guilt which might be associated with the feelings and with denying that they are present. It also creates an atmosphere of trust and openness between those involved. But, most of all it establishes a basis for finding some guidelines in the friendship. It is hard to overemphasize the importance of this stage in a friendship with someone of the opposite sex. I believe that unless opposite sex friends clearly establish guidelines at this point in their relationship, they are likely either to withdraw from each other or to rationalize their relationship until they do indeed become physically involved.

The responsibility for establishing guidelines in an opposite sex friendship rests with both friends. They will not only discuss the guidelines together, but they will freely discuss them with both their spouses. A few of the possible guidelines follow. First, it is important that neither of the opposite sex friends or their spouses assume anything. Rather than assume, things should always be checked out with the others. As an example, Ronda and Brent may both be planning to attend a state counseling convention in a neighboring city. Attendance involves spending two nights at the convention site. It would be easy to assume that they would drive together to the conference. But this assumption should be checked out with each other and in turn with each spouse.

Second, both friends should assume responsibility for physical control in the relationship. The tradition in our society has been for the man to be the sexual aggressor, while the woman sets the limits. This is part of the traditional double standard system in which sexual promiscuity is excused in males and condemned in females. This standard is inherently contradictory and hypocritical. Both the man and woman will control the physical limits in an opposite sex friendship.

Third, neither will sexually tease the other. Although both men and women engage in sexual teasing, the woman may be more skilled in this technique. Because women are not expected to be sexually aggressive, they are often tempted to resort to a type of sexual teasing in order to elicit attention from a male. There are numerous ways in which to flirt and tease sexually. Given the extent to which sexual teasing is utilized in advertising, virtually any girl by the time she has graduated from high school has mastered the art. Sexual teasing can take the form of a revealing neckline, a tight skirt, a tight sweater, a short skirt, a come-hither smile, an off-color joke, a sexual pun, etc. Most of us are conscious of our sexual teasing and flirtatious attempts. If, however, an innocent gesture is being wrongly interpreted as a sexual tease, this should be brought to the attention of the friend. Some persons are able to touch another very naturally, free of any sexual connotation.

Others, who have been reared in a physically restrictive background, may feel uncomfortable with much touching. To them, touching may have sexual connotations. Such differences can be expected and must be thoroughly discussed in the open as part of the guidelines.

Fourth, the friendship should always follow the lead of the person with the strongest felt limits. Take, for instance, the area of touch. If Ronda feels perfectly free and innocent in giving an embrace or hug, but Brent does not, they will agree to abide by Brent's limits. Or it may be that Ronda and Brent are contemplating traveling together by automobile to a distant counseling convention which requires an overnight stop on the way. Although they would have separate rooms in the motel, Ronda feels uncomfortable about the arrangement. In this case Brent will respect Ronda's limits. It goes without saying that married spouses will have full knowledge of any such arrangements and be in full accord. It may be that both Ronda and Brent feel comfortable with the traveling arrangement, but either Ronda's or Brent's spouse is not very enthusiastic over it. In this case Ronda and Brent will accept the limits of their spouses without any feelings of resentment or curtailment.

Not all situations will be as delicate as the example given here, but the guidelines can be applied in the same way.

INTELLECTUAL LEVEL

One of the greatest unrealistic and unnecessary burdens which we have placed upon the modern marriage relationship is the expectation that our spouse will fulfill all of our needs. We too often expect our husband or wife to be all things to us. The result is that the other feels inadequate when he or she can't meet all of our needs. A further result is jealousy when someone else is better able to fulfill just one dimension of our spouse's needs.

In our modern society each working spouse is likely to be involved in a very specialized form of work. In the past, when the majority of families were agricultural, both husband and wife were involved in the same type of economic activity. But today, husbands and wives often have very little actual knowledge of the details of their spouse's occupation. This means that because of occupational specialization, a high degree of intellectual sharing is possible in opposite sex friendships. It is within our occupational tasks that many of our creative energies gain expression. We admire and are drawn to others in our occupation who possess creative energies similar to our own. With the increased participation of women in all levels of employment, opposite sex friendships can be expected to develop on this basis.

Ronda, although a good counselor, may really admire the way Brent is able to conduct group counseling. She is more into individual counseling, and Brent has a real admiration for her skills in this area. They spend much time together at coffee breaks, over lunch, and even when they and their spouses get together, talking about counseling. There may develop a mutual admiration, an understanding between them on the intellectual level which is not as fully developed with their spouses. Is there any danger or undesirableness in this?

The degree of intellectual intimacy which can develop

between opposite sex friends is dependent upon the strength and health of the relationships between each friend and his and her spouse. If Ronda's husband happens to be a successful lawyer who is quite secure in his occupation and intellectual ability, he will likely be delighted in Ronda's intellectual intimacy with Brent. On the other hand, if he is really struggling professionally, and is unsure of his intellectual ability, he may very well be resentful of the positive affirmation which Brent is receiving from Ronda, but which he so desperately needs.

I am not suggesting that each spouse must be intellectually fulfilled by the other spouse in some academic way before they can tolerate an external intellectual intimacy on the part of their spouse. Let's suppose that Brent's wife completed her education at high school and then became a secretary before she met and married Brent. She now has three children, is a busy homemaker, but still finds time to lead a Girl Scout troop, and teach the eighth grade Sunday school class at church. She is creative in all her tasks and is receiving much positive reinforcement from others. She is secure enough in herself intellectually that she can encourage Brent in his intellectual intimacy with Ronda. If the marriage relationships are secure, I see no limits in intellectual intimacy which opposite sex friends can develeop.

EMOTIONAL INTIMACY

Emotional intimacy is the psychological and social dimension of a friendship. It involves two people feeling emotionally comfortable with each other. Emotional intimacy is experienced as total acceptance of the other, free from demands or expectations for change. Emotional intimacy is most central to the type of relationships discussed in this book. Friends will be free to express their feelings to each other.

Again however, the extent to which opposite sex friends will be able to become emotionally intimate will depend upon the nature of their marriage relationships. Ronda and Brent are counselors who are skilled in the art of human relating. They have developed empathetic skills, are trained to be sensitive to the needs and feelings of others, and know when and how to say a comforting or challenging word to other people. They are professional counselors who earn their living by their human relationship skills. If this is true, then is it not possible that Ronda and Brent are capable of establishing a more intimate emotional relationship with each other than either is able to establish with their spouses? Yes, this may be a very real possibility, which might become a danger to the marriage relationship.

However, the emotional intimacy between Ronda and Brent should allow them to share their enthusiasm for their spouses. Their emotional intimacy should allow them to see the other's spouse in the same light that their friend views them. They will be so close that they too come to love and appreciate the other's spouse. In this type of an emotional intimacy, the friendship is a contributing strength to the marriage relationship of each. Emotional intimacy should allow opposite sex friendships to be complementary instead of competitive to marriage relationships. If Ronda or Brent feels that either has a shortcoming in relating to their spouses, they can share this with each other, and by so doing help the other to develop into a more complete marriage partner.

Opposite Sex Friendships and Marriage

The second principle we gave for opposite sex friendships stated that commitment will be given to the friendship as long as it remains nonthreatening and secondary to the primary marital relationship of each spouse. This second principle has been implied throughout the foregoing discussion of the principle that physical, intellectual and emotional intimacy must be highly developed in both friends' marriage relationships before intimacy can develop in the friendship. If intimacy were to be greater in the friendship than in either's marriage relationship, there would be a real danger that the marriage would become the secondary relationship. Opposite sex friendships must always exist as a secondary relationship. Friends must be acutely aware of their own psychological needs and wants. They must be secure enough so that they will not allow their friendship to develop into a primary relationship. If a spouse is not receiving sufficient emotional intimacy, if basic psychological and social needs are not being met in the marriage relationship, then the development of an intimate opposite sex friendship is dangerous indeed. A decision at this point should involve limiting the friendship and establishing a stronger relationship in the marriage.

The development of opposite sex friendships is

desirable. They can be the source of rich human experiences and serve to strengthen the marriage relationship. *But,* they should be engaged in only by persons who already are a part of a loving, meaningful, intimate marriage relationship.

Should opposite sex friendships be avoided if one recognizes that his or her own marriage has its shortcomings? No, certainly not. But, one should be aware of one's vulnerability when the friendship promises to become more intimate than the marriage.

Till Inconvenience Do Us Part

Those of us who are fortunate enough to be a part of intimate opposite sex friendships must not get a false sense of their permanence. When we marry, we commit ourselves to our spouse for life—till death do us part. Our commitment in our opposite sex friend will continue as long as it works and positively contributes to our marriage relationship. The friendship can end when one friend moves away, finds another job, or changes to a degree that can't be tolerated by the other. Giving up an intimate friendship is not easy. It may not always be necessary, but sometimes we will need to give up being close to our friend. Then we should view the intimacy of friendship as a positive force which has caused personal growth and prepared us to establish these kinds of intimate friendships in the future.

A Personal Note

By this time you have realized, I'm sure, that in growing up I was very much the inexpressive male,

probably a cowboy type (see chapter 3). During my
high school and college days I found it hard to relate
closely to females. During my early high school days I
was apt to be a big tease—playfully pretending to steal
a book away from girls, splashing water on girls at the
swimming pool, or mockingly taunting the girls between classes. As I became an upper classman in high
school I attempted to emulate the strong silent male
type. I became very active in sports, pretending that I
did not have time for girls, when in fact I was rather
scared and uncomfortable to think of asking a girl out
for a date. I continued in this male role during my first
year in college. But as I became quite successful on the
college basketball team, I gradually edged into asking
girls out on dates. Although I was very popular with
both girls and guys, I still found it difficult to talk
freely to girls.

During my sophomore year in college I met Judy,
the girl who was to become my wife. I was on the
basketball team and Judy was a cheerleader, so we had
a common interest in sports, and it seemed only natural
that I should ask her out for a date. I soon found that
Judy was a little different than most of the girls I had
known. She seemed to be genuinely interested in what
I had to say. She was free to talk about her feelings,
and she nonforcefully asked me how I was feeling about
certain things. Judy became the first woman with whom
I was able to establish a close, sharing, intimate relationship. As our relationship has grown over the years,
my ability to establish opposite sex friendships has also

developed. Let me tell you about my friendship with a woman I will fictitiously call Jill (although I'm sure that neither she nor her husband would object to being identified in this book; both in fact have read what follows).

I first met Jill when she was an undergraduate student at a college where I was teaching. As a student she was intelligent and creative, the type of student who makes teaching rewarding. From the beginning Judy knew of my enthusiasm for Jill's ability as a student. And to think she even wanted to become a sociologist too! Jill became a very close friend to both Judy and me.

Between Jill's junior and senior year I left the college to teach at the University of Georgia. I continued to correspond with Jill and advised her on applying to graduate programs in sociology, as she was determined to become a sociologist. Due to her outstanding undergraduate record, Jill was accepted by several outstanding graduate sociology programs. As it turned out, she decided to come to the University of Georgia.

Although Jill renewed her friendship with Judy and me after she got here, she soon began to question her purpose in life and the meaning of existence. This was taking place during the height of the student counterculture movement, and Jill experimented with drugs, Eastern mysticism, and generally adopted the counterculture lifestyle, as did many college students at that time. I can remember once receiving a phone call in the middle of the night. It was Jill crying, desperately

lonely and afraid, largely due to the effects of drugs. I
went to get her and brought her back to our home where
Judy and I comforted her until she could go to sleep.

One day Jill came into my office at school and began
to cry, revealing her present confusion as to what life
was all about. I felt very inadequate at the time. As I
remember, I told her that I believed that meaning in
life was centered in a personal relationship with Jesus
Christ. I then assured her that there was a God who
really loved her, and that I too loved her. I cried as well,
because I cared about the desperate loneliness and tur-
moil she was experiencing at that time.

Through her personal searching and reading of the
Bible, Jill came to a personal relationship with Jesus
Christ. She didn't tell me of this until two months after
her decision, still uncertain of the implications of her
new-found faith. With both of us committed to the
lordship of Jesus Christ in our lives, our relationship
proceeded on a firmer foundation. She and I had a
special relationship. Perhaps I was in part a father substitute (her father had died when she was very young).
It was important for her to feel loved by me as a man
and also to be able to grapple with difficult questions
about meaning in life and the relationship between
Christianity and sociology. The relationship was important to me too, because it was proving to me that I
could be a part of an intimate friendship with a woman
other than my wife. This was made possible because Jill
also felt close to Judy and to us as a couple.

Jill now has her doctor's degree and is a college sociology professor. She is also married and the mother of

two children. Jill's husband Rick, is a very warm expressive person, more so than I am, and I count him as one of my very closest male friends. Judy is as close to Rick as I am to Jill and counts herself equally close to both Rick and Jill. As I think about the degree of closeness the four of us have been able to achieve, it seems to me the key has been that each of us is first of all committed to the lordship of Jesus Christ in our lives. Second, we are committed to our spouses and the primacy of our marriage relationship. And third, we are committed to each other as persons, based upon the strength of the first two commitments.

NOTES

1. Sheila Kessler and Jack Clarke, "Createmates," in *The Personnel and Guidance Journal* 55, no. 1 (Sept. 1976): 37–39.

9

Why God *Can* Say
"I Love You"

IN THE PREVIOUS chapters we have been concerned with
the ability of people to express love in intimate relationships. One of the themes of this book has been that
the free expression of love is hindered by fear. We
often do not say "I love you" because we are afraid. We
are afraid not just of revealing our feelings *for* that
person, but because the revelation of our love makes us
vulnerable; it is possible that our expression of love
will be rejected.

There is one never-failing source of love for each of
us, who never has trouble saying "I love you"—God.
Why can God say "I love you" to us? The apostle John
gives us insight into this question when he says, "God
is love. There is no fear in love, but perfect love casts
out fears" (1 John 4:16, 18). God can express love because he is perfect love. He can say, "I love you," because he does not fear rejection. Notice, however, that
this is not to say that God does not expect rejection.

God knew from the beginning that he was creating beings who not only could but would reject him.

God can perfectly express love because of his perfect nature. We stumble in our attempts to express love because of our imperfect nature. Our nature is stained by sin. We are beings who are self-oriented—whose natural inclination is to look out for ourselves first. We were created in the image of God, but because of sin—both the original sin of Adam and our own—that image was shattered. However, we still have the image of God within us, regardless of how shattered it may be. In our natural state we want to love, to show love, to express love. But our fallen human nature keeps getting in the way.

Our human love is conditional love. It is love that says "I love you *because* you love me," or "I will love you *if* you will love me." That is, it is conditioned on either a prior love or an expected response of love. With the Apostle John we can only say, "We love him because he first loved us" (1 John 4:19, KJV).

God's love is unconditional love. The Apostle John also described this love when he said, "In this is love, not that we loved God but that he loved us" (1 John 4:10). God's unconditional love simply says "I love you," without needing to be assured of our prior love or demanding our response of love. Unconditional love is perfect love and only God's love is perfect. His unconditional perfect love moved him to give himself for us. "For God so loved the world that he gave his only Son" (John 3:16). We are God's love objects. The giving of God of his Son Jesus is not dependent upon a proper response in us. God loved us before we loved him, and he loves us whether we love him in return or not.

How are we, as imperfect beings, capable of attaining perfect love that will free us to make an unconditional statement like "I love you"? The answer is tied up in our response to God's offer of unconditional love. God unconditionally gave his Son Jesus Christ as the perfect offering or sacrifice for our sins. Our sins, or more correctly, our sinful nature is what has kept us bound and unable to offer our love unconditionally to others. Although we were created by God and for God, each of us, because of our tainted sin nature, is in a state of rebellion from God. In reality, God gave his Son to reclaim us, although we were already his by right. The death of Jesus on the cross was a redeeming act which paid the penalty for our sins—which "purchased" us for God.

Jesus gave his life for us so that we might have abundant and overflowing life. And that involves the ability to love perfectly and to be free from the bondage to sin and self-centeredness. This thought is captured in Jesus' words, "You will know the truth, and the truth will make you free" (John 8:32). Paul captures this same thought in Galatians 5:1 when he says, "It was for freedom that Christ set us free; therefore keep standing firm and do not be subject again to a yoke of slavery" (NAS).

We cannot realize the freedom which can be gained from God's offer of unconditional love, however, unless we accept it. This freedom cannot be earned. This promise of new life, eternal life, is ours for the taking. We need only to give up our life of bondage to sin, and accept a new life of freedom by claiming Jesus Christ as our Lord and Savior.

Jesus Christ as God and Man

God supremely revealed himself in Jesus Christ, who lived his life on this earth both totally God and totally man. Through the ages people have had trouble conceiving of the two natures, the human and the divine, dwelling in the one person of Jesus Christ. Theologically this has led, on the one hand, to minimizing Jesus' humanity and magnifying his divinity, and on the other to magnifying his humanity and minimizing his divinity. Those who minimize the humanity of Jesus, see him as God only disguised as man. He looked, acted, and seemed to be a man, but he was not really subject to the limitations and problems of human existence. Such a view produces a cold and remote Jesus, whom we can hardly believe will sympathize with us in all our infirmities.

Those who magnify the humanity of Jesus see him as not too different from any other man. Jesus becomes the "man upstairs," a "superstar," or as once described by a famous movie star, a "living doll." Jesus becomes so crassly human as scarcely to command our highest reverence.

A corresponding perversion of the true character of Jesus is to see him either as the embodiment of masculinity or the embodiment of femininity. Throughout history the feminine characteristics of Jesus have often been emphasized, so that Jesus becomes a meek, soft-spoken, kindly person, who has about as much backbone as a wet noodle. One reaction to this view is the temptation to create a masculine Jesus, who was rough, strong, demanding, and a fierce leader of men.

The Emotional Life of Jesus

What was Jesus really like emotionally? If we take a look at the total life of Jesus, we see a man who experienced a wide range of emotions. The most dominant emotion was his compassion or love. The four Gospels report numerous occasions in which Jesus showed both internal feelings (he loved and pitied) and external action (he relieved pain and suffering). His love is seen in his relationships with other individuals such as the blind man, lepers, the bereaved widow, the woman at the well of Sychar, and the mourners of dead Lazarus. His compassion and love for the multitudes can be seen in his acts of feeding them, healing them, and expressing distress about their lostness in describing them as "sheep without a shepherd."

Jesus' compassion and love was expressed also in emotions of sorrow and joy. He was moved to weeping over the unbelief of Jerusalem. When he saw Mary and her friends weeping at Lazarus' death, he too wept. In healing the deaf and dumb man, Jesus looked up to heaven with a deep sigh. When the Pharisees wanted to test him by asking for a sign from heaven, he sighed deeply.

At other times the love of Jesus moved him to express great joy. When the seventy disciples whom he had sent out to witness for him returned rejoicing, we are told that Jesus "rejoiced greatly in the Holy Spirit" (Luke 10:21, NAS). He also speaks of joy in heaven when just one sinner repents (Luke 15:7). He tells his disciples that if they will abide in his love, then his joy will also be in them (John 15:10–11). The love of Jesus toward his disciples can also be seen in his statements to them as he prepares to leave them: "for the moment you are sad at heart; but I shall see you again, and then you will be joyful, and no one shall rob you of your joy" (John 16:22, NEB). In praying to his heavenly Father, Jesus shows his compassion for mankind by saying that he has spoken his truth so that men might be filled with joy (John 17:13).

Although Jesus was meek, mild, and tender, he was also capable of anger and indignation. In a world under the curse of sin, the emotions of anger and righteous indignation were Jesus' response to man's inhumanity to man, to man's hardness of heart and unbelief, and to man's acts of hypocrisy. The same Jesus who said, "Suffer the little children to come unto me," went into the temple and drove out the buyers and sellers and upset the tables of the money-changers with a whip. Jesus' anger at the hypocrisy of the Pharisees can be seen in his calling them "tombs covered with whitewash . . . full of dead men's bones and all kinds of filth," "snakes," and "vipers' brood" (Matt. 23:27, 33, NEB). His language was equally severe when he called Herod "a fox," those unreceptive of his message "swine," and false prophets "savage wolves."

In his humanity, Jesus possessed a wide range of emotions and was harmoniously complete in his own individuality. He also has the full range of human needs and appetites as he hungered, thirsted, was weary, knew physical pain and pleasure, slept, grew in knowledge, wept, suffered, and died. All that is human manifested itself in perfect proportion and balance in Jesus Christ. Jesus was emotionally mature and able to freely express and show his emotions to himself and to others.

Peter, Do You Love Me?

In the last chapter of his Gospel, John gives an account of one of the last exchanges between Jesus and his disciples. Peter and some of the other disciples have been fishing during the night on the sea of Galilee. They come to shore just as day is breaking, and find Jesus with a charcoal fire ready, inviting them to join him in breakfast. The breakfast leads to Jesus' curious quizzing of Peter's love for him. Three times Jesus asks Peter, "Do you love me?" After each question Peter replies, "Yes, you know that I love you." We are told that Peter was grieved after Jesus asked him this question the third time.

Although there is no way to know the mind of Jesus during this encounter, we know that he had a definite reason for posing the same question to Peter three times. It may be more than coincidental that Peter had earlier denied Jesus three times. Perhaps now Jesus was giving Peter the opportunity to assert what he had previously denied—and in as many times. We have no way of knowing whether Peter to this point had asked Jesus' forgiveness for his denial. If he had not, this incident can be taken as an example of how Jesus encouraged Peter to express his feelings of love. Perhaps Peter had a definite need to express these feelings, to reaffirm his love after it had been denied through his actions. Jesus knew that soon Peter would be one of a small group left on this earth to carry on the work which He had started. Peter needed a chance to recommit himself to Jesus and affirm his love. After the incident Peter was a changed person. The person who traveled throughout the then known world telling the good news of Jesus' victory over death, was hardly reminiscent of the person who just a short time earlier had denied Jesus three times.

Each of Us Can Be Changed Persons

Peter changed from an intimidated coward during Christ's crucifixion, to a fearless witness after Jesus' ascension. We, too, can change from living fearful lives, in which we are afraid of telling others how we feel about them, to persons who are secure in who we are because we are personally related to the Creator of the universe. In knowing why God can say "I love you," we can know how we can say "I love you."

> *There is no fear in love, but perfect love casts out fear.*
> *For fear has to do with punishment, and he who fears is*
> *not perfect in love.*
> *We love, because he first loved us.*
> *1 John 4:18–19*